MAKING IT HOME

MAKING IT HOME

Europe and the Politics of Culture

SIMON MUNDY

European Cultural Foundation

Published by the European Cultural Foundation
Jan van Goyenkade 5,
NL-1075 HN AMSTERDAM
Tel. 00 31 20 676 0222

Produced by Parapress, 12 Dene Way, Speldhurst, Kent TN3 0NX

ISBN 1-898594-40-6

Printed and bound in Great Britain by
Biddles Ltd, Guildford and King's Lynn

By the Same Author

Poetry
Letter to Carolina
By Fax to Alice Springs

Music
Elgar
The Children's Story of Music
Alexander Glazunov
Bernard Haitink: A Working Life
Purcell

For Bruce Jenks,
through whom I first came to appreciate
international organizations

Contents

Foreword

As we leave the twentieth century and prepare to enter the twenty-first, Europe is struggling to define its future and its place in the world. It faces a series of major dialectic dilemmas which pit, for example, unity against diversity, continuity against change, allegiance against flexibility and common consciousness against self-determination.

Europe has a single market and may yet have a single currency. It is well on the road to providing common political and social rights for its citizens, although this goal is a long way from being achieved. The Europe of the future, however, cannot be defined only by the opportunity and the right to purchase across the length and breadth of Europe the same goods at the same prices with the same banknotes. Nor can it be defined by the chance to live and work everywhere under the same legal and social conditions, which would nonetheless be one of the great achievements of our history.

Europe is about much, much more. Heritage and history have cultivated the European soil, producing ideals and values which have not only been disseminated in Europe but all over the world. Simon Mundy detects the existence of an extraordinary continuity. He questions a European policy which ignores these deeper dimensions that have shaped European mentalities (and which cannot be attained either by the market and monetary strategies or by political compromises or military co-operation). Europe cannot exist without developing a politics of culture, without enshrining cultural rights and promoting cultural action. Culture is the bedrock of Europe, according to Simon Mundy, and he makes the telling point that, 'a union which fails to win over hearts as well as wallets will not survive.'

Europe needs strong voices to remind us all that Europe is more than a single market and a single currency. We need those voices to proclaim that the future of our continent depends upon our will and our love, our minds and our hearts.

Simon Mundy's is just such a voice and we believe he should be heard. His essay is not a message in a bottle to be tossed into the wild seas of dispute around Europe and then forgotten until it is washed up on shore years later. We hope it will become a trail-blazer which with bring in its wake a widespread debate about the importance of culture in Europe. That is firmly our intention – the European Cultural Foundation has long been concerned with raising awareness of cultural issues on a European level and promoting culture as a ferment for developing European society.

Simon Mundy's voice is a British voice for Europe as well as a European voice for Britain. And not only for Britain but for all people in Europe who are engaging and opting for a common destiny. His voice is not that of the European Cultural Foundation, it is a voice that we ourselves find provocative and stimulating. We are pleased and proud to offer him a platform from which to address Europe's citizens.

Dr Rüdiger Stephan,
Secretary-General,
European Cultural Foundation

Preface

To write about the culture that informs European political life is a pleasure and a fascination at any time. To write about it at a moment when the continent is grappling to come to terms with the remnants of its empires, the collapse of Soviet power, the struggle to rebuild Eastern European nations as prosperous liberal democracies, is a duty too. It is a moment when those territories which comprise Western Europe are reverting to their old power politics: balancing France and Germany and trying to avoid political and economic domination from either. And it is a moment when many are wondering if merging currencies to form a means of exchange as effete-sounding as the Euro will be worth the concentration of wealth along the Rhine and the loss of self-determination that will follow. Making it home means creating a Europe which feels like home for all its citizens, without making it a home barren of its rich character, shaped by a history that is chaotic and vicious but consistently inspiring too. Making it home is also as much a hope as an aspiration. In all of this culture in its broadest definition is the emotional motor both of unification and of opposition to it. Culture in its more limited definition – of people's expressive activity – is the least favoured or politically powerful aspect of life in any of Europe's nations. I was encouraged to be polemical in my approach, for although culture can inspire some fine flights of rhetoric it is also prone to be discussed in the deadest terms of sociological and managerial jargon. To avoid that I have not been afraid to be at times personal and provocative, even to stretch the conventional readings of history without, I hope, being inaccurate or unreasonable. If there is a purpose it is to stimulate open debate about an area which political pragmatists prefer to leave as quiet as they can.

It is a privilege to have been given this opportunity and I must thank a few for it: Dr Rüdiger Stephan and Odile Chenal of the

European Cultural Foundation for providing the means; for their discussion and encouragement, through which many of the ideas that follow have been developed, Raymond Georis, the former Secretary-General of the ECF, Helena Vaz da Silva MEP, Raymond Weber and Gabriele Mazza of the Council of Europe, Ferdinand Richard of the European Forum for the Arts and Heritage and Alexander Schischlik of UNESCO. My thanks also to Jo Shapcott for vetting the manuscript and removing the occasional uncharitable jibe.

Simon Mundy,
Gladestry,
Wales, January 1977

I

Divide and Collide

'... this land is not the sweet home that it looks,
   Nor its peace the historical calm of a site
Where something was settled once and for all ...'

W.H. Auden
In Praise of Limestone

The geology of Europe is a violent story of lands rising from the sea, sinking and rising again only to be tipped and crushed by plates from the south and west; of volcanic rifts and fissures blasting through the gentle sediments; of glaciers that reduce Himalayan ranges to Cambrian hills, of young mountains and old valleys. Europe's lands have never quite settled down and neither have their peoples. Just as the landscape has moved in a series of major transformations and been shaped in between by the smaller but insidiously effective dividing forces of morphology, so the human movements have been characterized in the last four thousand years by an almost geological response to settlement and political organization. The five main groupings of people, Latins, Celts, Teutons, Norse and Slavs, have subjected each other to violent social convulsions interspersed with calmer periods when the distinctions between each have been shaped by more local (though often no less vicious) forces.

Now and then one or more of these peoples has come to the conclusion that Europe needs to be controlled in a less haphazard fashion. The natural feeling of each group that their means of government, trade, inheritance, expression and land use was the best available led them to want to see the continent organized accordingly. Greed and domination were only ever half the story. The other half was a sense of incomprehension that other people, usually those being displaced or subjugated, could not see the reasonableness, the plain logic, of the exercise. Conquest was followed by cultural superimposition, a pie crust holding in the very different ingredients in the hope that if they were cooked together long enough under sufficient pressure they would blend and amalgamate into a satisfyingly homogenous dish.

Now and then it seemed to be possible. For a while each seemed to be achieving a form of stability. First the Celts in the west and the Slavs in the east, then the Latins pushing up from the south. For the last sixteen hundred years it has been the Germanic tribes, the Teutons and Norse, who have been convinced that they were best placed to impose their version of order on the continent. Logically, being settled geographically in the central belt of the land mass, sometimes in a narrow band, sometimes in one which confined others to the fringes, they saw theirs as the pivotal and therefore the naturally most significant role. Their division into four linked but competing elements of Franks, Germans, English and Scandinavians has not changed that fundamental perception. Which of the four elements had the right to be dominant within that overall assumption has been the basic question that has shaped the politics of the region so ferociously since the fragmentation of the Roman empire. To a large extent the other peoples of the continent have been forced into the service of this debate – if debate is not too kindly a word for the cruelty with which the argument has been presented. Either they have become subordinated to Germanic aristocratic classes or, more recently, they have had no option but to define themselves economically only in relation to the Germanic markets. The same of course was true of the Latin expansion under Rome and no doubt before that under the Celtic domination – though the cultural tradition of the pre-Christian Celts, which opposed the written record of the language, has meant that our understanding of it has had to rely on archaeology more than for other empires of the period (in the middle east or China, for example).

In the short time since the Second World war, the last and most convulsive of all these attempts at overall control, there has emerged a consensus that the argument is starting to be not only exhausting and wasteful of the resources (human and natural) of the continent but increasingly absurd in a period when, five hundred years after empirically noticing it for the first time, Europeans are finally realising that they occupy an uncomfortably small part of the world. For much of that five hundred years Europe managed to ignore the fact by exporting its people (and with them its political arguments) to almost everywhere else. By being so self-destructive through two all-embracing wars within a few years, however, Europeans have lost that ability and the economic authority that went with it. For a time, until 1990, Western Europeans and the post-colonial nations they had founded were offered the consuming prospect of a splendidly distracting alternative in the Cold War, a confrontation between the Slavs and themselves in which they could claim an engaging interest. That in one sense proved useful. It allowed the fragmented nations of Western Europe time and reason to explore a different path.

At last there is a sense among all the ethnic and cultural factions that Europe's differences are irrelevant to future prosperity and influence. There is agreement that political convergence and economic convergence not only go together but are inevitable unless the world order collapses completely. The majority of politicians are realistic enough to know, however, that while differences must be minimized they cannot be ignored. Instead a constructive way must be found to use difference so that no one ethnic group or territorial entity dominates, while at the same time allowing enough leeway for each people to pursue traditional (and by now surely genetic) interests.

The Germanic tribes of Europe have been at the centre of the building and demolition of Europe for over two thousand years, dominating it for the last fifteen hundred. The term Germanic, understood by classical politicians as early as the first century AD, applies not just to those that call themselves or speak German but to the group of tribes that came to form most of the nations of northern Europe. The Ostrogoths and Visigoths who so troubled Rome were perhaps the first to be identified as such. Then it came to include the Vikings, Norse, Franks and Saxons and the rest of the complicated mix of tribes that occupied the land cornered by the Rhine and the Danube and all that lay to the north-east, translating into Scandinavians (without most Finns), the Dutch, English, French, Germans and the Austrians.

They have always pursued their territorial goals with enthusiasm but not always with great finesse. This was as true of the British and French empires as it was of the Visigothic, Viking and Frankish invasions. Distance was rarely a dissuading factor. Whereas the Slavs and the Mediterranean peoples tended to conquer adjacent territory, gradually extending the lands they controlled by spreading outward from the centre, the Germanic peoples progressed by despatching marauding bands whose instructions, or at least whose instincts, were to range as far as possible. They expected little reinforcement but were confident of their own ability to survive in a hostile country where, sooner or later, they would have established a firm enough foothold to be able to offer a home to other bands coming in their direction. This pattern was followed consistently, if sometimes unconsciously, from the Saxon incursions into Celtic Britain in the fifth century and the Viking probes to Ireland and Newfoundland in the eighth, to the explorations of Van Diemen and Captain Cook in the eighteenth and on into the major period of European empire building, which was only brought to a halt by the First World War. Even the Spanish conquest of the Americas falls into this category, for although the initial exploration was undertaken by sailors like Magellan and Columbus from ports under Iberian or Italian control, the real colonization only really took root once the Hapsburgs established their rule south of the Alps and Pyrenees.

There was another peculiar characteristic of the Germanic peoples that was only present to a lesser extent in the Slavs and Latins. This was the fierce loyalty that invaders developed to the lands they had conquered, a loyalty that within a few generations supplanted the consciousness of the original home territory. Not only did they soon regard the new territory as home, they expropriated the myths of the previous inhabitants and built up a pedigree for themselves which either legitimized their presence in the new colony or which obliterated from conscious recognition the previous existence of the country. The Normans are a good case in point. Very soon after their arrival as Norse invaders on the north west coast of the continent they regarded themselves as indigenous to the area. The Saxons and Danes, meanwhile, had pulled off the same psychological trick in southern Britain, establishing it as England from 973 AD. When ninety years later the Norman Dukes overthrew their Saxon cousins, they quickly assumed an absolute right as a local ruling class, within two centuries regarding England as more important to retain than Normandy. So complete was the illusion that children in English schools are still taught to regard history as having begun properly with the Norman invasion in 1066, anything previous to that being looked on either as 'ancient history' or 'the dark ages'.

At much the same time the Franks were pursuing a similar course further south. They quickly separated themselves from Charlemagne's attempt to bring together a new version of the Roman empire and began to consolidate around the Isle de France. It was a long process, taking them until the end of the sixteenth century to establish undisputed control of the whole of modern France. Nonetheless a myth of nationhood encompassing the whole area was used to justify their ambition from remarkably early in the process.

The Franks and the Normans differed in one important aspect from the majority of other colonising tribes in Europe after the sixth century: the way they developed language. Whereas the Germanic and Norse tongues remained firmly in use across the central belt of Europe, the Franks and Normans expropriated the majority of their languages from the new areas they inhabited. Norman Frankish, the ruling tongue in England until the middle of the fourteenth century, was gradually dropped in favour of English, the Saxon-dominated hybrid that emerged with a strong element of Latin. The Franks themselves opted for an even stronger Latin recipe which abandoned much of the Germanic vocabulary but retained a great deal of complicated Frankish grammar.

Other groups took their language with them and stuck to it: the British Celts settling Brittany, the Gallic Celts invading Northern Britain (replacing the British-speaking Picts), the Norse in Shetland, Iceland and Orkney, the Slavs re-establishing themselves in the Celtic heartland between the Danube and the

Vltava, the Balts and Magyar settling between the Germanic and Slav demesnes.

With all the zeal of converts, though, the Franks and Normans, as they redefined themselves as French and upper class English, came to regard all other languages and dialects spoken on their territory as abnormal and dangerous. In France it is an attitude that is still reflected in cultural policy (under the right-wing administrations of the mid-1990s the Ministry for Culture underlined the point by insisting on the word Francophone in the title). Only in very recent years have the regional languages of the country been regarded as anything other than pestilential and deserving of abolition. There is still no television in Alsatian, Breton, Occitans or Basque and to be heard speaking these languages is regarded by most French as rather uncivilized, certainly lacking any cosmopolitan flair. England has been partially more enlightened but only in the last twenty-five years. The Norman aristocracy still derides regional dialects and, until well after the Second World War, penalized Celtic languages with extraordinary vindictiveness. Cornish and Manx were entirely wiped out. Scots and Irish Gaelic and the old British Celtic (which the English labelled Welsh, derived from the Saxon word for foreigner; a piece of cultural double-dealing which demonstrates the attitude perfectly) were beaten back to the most western peninsulas of the continent. With varying degrees of imposition the same policy was followed by both nations as they expanded into the Americas, Africa and Asia. The height, or perhaps the depth, of absurdity was reached when these Germanic tribes encountered each other competitively far across the world; English against Dutch in South Africa, English against French in Canada and Louisiana, French against English in parts of the West Indies.

In many ways it was a brilliant policy, learned perhaps from the Romans. Through power the language was spread. Now, with the military and most of the political power relinquished, language remains to exert influence. Within Europe French, English and German (in that order) dominate the exchange of ideas and therefore the thinking that is adopted. As a result of Germany's two disastrous war initiatives in 1914 and 1939 it has lost the linguistic coverage it once enjoyed, but this may change as it manoeuvres to be at the centre of the new Franco-German economic empire under construction. Outside Europe, English and French, with large pools of Spanish left over from the Hapsburg empire, are assured of a dominant place by becoming the languages of air travel, computer technology and the most successful exporters of entertainment.

After one and a half thousand years of competition at every level, finding a peaceful and progressive path upon which all Europeans can travel with confidence has not been easy. The arrogance of the larger countries (even when they are in a period of low self-confidence) towards smaller countries and regional nations within their own borders, puts many of their fine intentions in jeopardy. It is an arrogance born of centuries of believing that other people and their cultures are mere curiosities, often worth preserving in a museum like the last specimen of a rare orchid, but hardly worth considering in the world of real politics. Where land is exploitable then competition for financial reward brings an extra degree of attention but not real concern. Where there is concern it is for the protection of assets and influence. Consequently countries which are intrinsically no more impressive than others in terms of size or contribution to the world become disproportionately important in international politics.

America, one of the first places where Europe fought its proxy wars, has learned well from its founders. Paradoxically its concerns are governed by a strange sort of reverse colonialism. Those countries which have sent large numbers of people to settle in America – mainly as a result of conflict between the European nations or because of their attitude to other peoples in their own territory – receive an unusually high degree of attention, finance and involvement from the world's most successful economy. So Israel and Ireland, two countries of similar population, are central to the emotional drive of American foreign policy. The fact that they are the same size as Swaziland and have much the same number of inhabitants as Arizona cannot diminish their cause. Maybe the case should be put the other way round. If Swaziland and the native American people of Arizona received the same level of investment and attention from Washington that Israel and Ireland do, the world might be a more rational and less bitter place. How long America will remain the world's dominant state is another matter. The likelihood is that in a few years China will be competing for that position. Its traditions are to regard the outside world, and indeed the views of its own people, as irrelevant and contemptible, a prospect which makes its emergence even less appetising than the colonial period or the Cold War.

The arrogance shown by the larger European nations is having two consequences in the post-cold war period. Both are making more difficult the twin goals of European harmony (but not harmonization, as I shall explain later) and a world free of ethnic conflict. In European terms the principle of national state-hood, the inevitable result of several centuries of increasingly centralized authority in the dominant European groups, has institutionalized the belief that peoples not defined by statehood are unimportant. At the same time there is a tacit belief that while small states are useful to make the policies of the big states legitimate through building a majority, they are only really there to give a veneer of credibility to the idea of a Europe of equals. The old European game of building diplomatic alliances to block one or other major state becoming too powerful has not changed. If the potential alliance is between France and Germany, then England aims for a balancing role. If Spain and France are acting jointly, Italy reacts. If the Mediterranean countries work together, the northern ones are watchful. For four hundred years Europe's politics have been governed by one crucial question: are France and Germany – whatever their internal constitutional arrangements – working with or against each other ? If the answer is with, then there is a real fear that all other areas of Europe will only be able to operate by reference to this central geographical and economic polity. If against, then the fear is that every-body else will have to take sides and the result will be, at worst, war, at best political stagnation and commercial decline.

The second eventuality is still apparent in those countries and areas of the world where European colonization's legacy is unresolved. The period of colonial rule varied immensely. In some places, especially in parts of Africa and South-East Asia, it was surprisingly short: not much more than fifty years, with much of that taken up by declining interest and authority because of the two world wars. They were only world wars in the first place because they coincided with the period of maximum imperial rule (Japan's opportunist attempts to build an empire for itself very late in the day emphasizes the point).

For those places where colonialism dates back three or more hundred years, the pattern was different. By the time that the newer countries were being carved out to complete the empires, the older settlements – like the British Dominions, the United States, Mexico, Brazil, Argentina – had already achieved either full independence or at least the trappings of home rule. This of course was home rule for the settlers, not the original inhabitants. In almost all the countries established in the first two centuries of colonization the native people were not merely subjugated but either wiped out entirely or confined to wilderness or marginal land and allowed few rights in the emerging nations. For Australia, New Zealand, South Africa, Brazil and Central America the issues arising from this still resonate through the political consciousness.

For those countries in the later, nineteenth- and early twentieth-century phases of colonization, however, the pattern was different. Here the local population was harassed but not displaced. Often local political structures were left intact but had a new governing layer placed over them. While plainly better than old fashioned genocide, the new 'national' structures, carved out between European nations using a bad map and a straight ruler, took no account of traditional boundaries, dividing true ethnic nations between several countries and utterly disregarding great regional kingdoms like the Ashanti. Where the colonial powers did recognize the tribal realities they often exacerbated the existing antagonisms, as the French did between the Hutus and Tutsis in Central Africa and the British did between the Shona and Mtabele further south. The use of the word tribe is itself indicative. When Europeans regarded people as inferior or as anthropological curiosities they were tribes. When they were seen as equals, basically other Europeans or the derivatives, they were accorded the title of nations.

11

Forty years after colonialism collapsed the real nations are starting to take back control and the imposed state structures are either falling apart or coming to be dominated by one of the old pre-colonial elites. The tribal governments of Europe – France, Britain, Belgium, Portugal and Germany – gaze at the result with mixed emotions. The mix combines a measure of guilt with a greater measure of helplessness. The urge to do something is tempered by the desire not to make the same assumptions of superiority as the colonial generations. Yet this generation may respond by going too far in the opposite direction. It may reduce itself to hand-wringing inaction, replacing outward greed and exploitation with inward-looking self-indulgence and the comfort of penitential inertia.

The direction taken by the perpetrators of colonialism is now double-headed. One head leads towards a sublimation of all the warlike and aggressive characteristics which have epitomized Europeans for the last two millennia. White liberal (mostly of European settler stock) Americans become introverted, isolationist and, at home, hypersensitive to any personal remarks that suggest difference or imply social failings. Words, however innocently intended, are seen always to be weapons in the hands of others who have the perceived potential to cause fear or who, collectively, are regarded as being responsible for a person's lack of advancement and self-esteem. This parade of grievance, even more this exhibition of militant weakness, is in danger of clogging the law courts, paralysing freedom of discussion in universities and reducing politics to the profession of quack doctor; dispensing palliatives for diseases beyond its understanding. Instead the sensitivity should be turned by social conscience into action, devising common programmes which develop benefits collectively which cannot be delivered personally. In America this rarely happens. The society, in coping with its legacy of tainted dreams, asks its public institutions to combine the virtue of the vestal virgin with the transforming power of Merlin. When the vestiges of old military muscle are exhibited in an operation beyond their borders the terrified citizens can come to terms with them only if there is no cost in lives on their own side; if there are no expendable extras supporting the show's stars. The military might has

12

to deliver an absolute victory as clean and stainless as the disinfectant in the kitchen sink.

If this condition is spreading to Europe, mostly via Britain and Holland, we should not be surprised. America was a European invention and its peculiarities and problems come home like prodigals. In Europe itself the manifestations so far are different and are evident more among the politicians and the journalists who commentate on them than among the voters. Realising that no nation in the area has the means or the political will to operate with the old arrogance and imperial posturing, but equally realising that having caused or inflamed many of the disputes around the world there is a responsible role to play, Europe's leaders quarrel instead about degrees of involvement, lines of command and the difference between imposing order for humanitarian and political reasons, as though it was possible to separate one from another. Somebody has to lead, but no country will accept the responsibility and if it did (as France tends to assume it can now and again), such leadership would be unacceptable to the others. We are all equal and if some are more equal than others they must at least have the decency not to show it.

* * *

While the agonising over the shape of imperial countries in a post-imperial world prevents coherent policy emerging, in Europe itself the original six members of the European Community do their best to pretend that the only way to escape from their war-torn past is to sublimate all traces of administrative difference. The idea is not that all bureaucracies and political processes should be the same – the idea of Italian, French and German official machinery working in unison is plainly ridiculous – rather it is that they should operate under precisely the same laws. This leaves the political process too often incapable of independent action by any one nation and too conscious of internal priorities to do anything effective jointly. The assumption is that only by this technocratic abasement of character can Europe remain at peace.

This is a technocratic vision of unity. It stems fundamentally from the need felt by officials to take action while being able to share or shift blame for the result. It hankers after a world in which order is obvious and unquestioned. It places its faith in paper rules and the ability of government to forbid. Directives and resolutions, judgements and opinions, regulations and instructions will succeed where political instinct and personal variety has failed. In one sense though the spirit of the colonizer is still alive, even if its energy is directed towards home or near home. Order can only be seen to be intact if the mechanisms to enforce it are in the control of one national tradition or one supplemented by pliant allies. Bureaucratic order can only be sustained through economic and political control. In their desperate desire to be part of that order politicians, aware of their own limitations and anxious not to seem part of the discredited orthodoxies of the past, are willing to cede control to unelected officials in the name of modernity, inter-dependence and – the biggest sweetener of all – peace.

This though, is a dark view of European political motivation. Many of the policies which have arisen as a result of post-colonial reassessment are sensible and well-balanced. In a world where trading relationships and technological innovation far outstrip the pace of governmental development, bureaucratic order is sometimes the best that can be achieved in the short-term.

Of course, the trouble is that we are always in the short-term, an aspect of reality which the political life-cycles of European democracies accentuate. Even when governments remain in power for well over a decade, allowing a measure of continuity in policy, the details of that policy are altered (not always with much subtlety) by the proximity of elections. In a community of democratic nations such as the European Union, there is always going to be one important partner whose preoccupation is with the imminence of political oblivion and who cannot be relied upon to take an entirely far-sighted view. This is a useful brake on political adventurers but it also means that those seeking re-election will blame Europe for any failings and amplify their own ability to influence change. The result is always disappointment. Fellow leaders feel betrayed as cherished projects are delayed. Populations see themselves betrayed as their 'national interests', as defined by the political establishment desperate for preservation, are ignored or dismissed as secondary by the dominant partners in the collective.

Despite all this the measure of agreement is surprisingly broad. Europe is a small area. Had it been Europe that had been colonized, rather than Africa, it (excluding the former Soviet Union countries) would now be seen as comparable to Zaire in size and half that of India in population. It is worth making such a jump in perception for a moment. In terms of land use it is clearly absurd not to regard Europe as broadly one economic system with a reliably coherent approach to the outside world. This is what North American and Far Eastern countries increasingly expect of us and what we expect of similar sized conurbations of nations. India, with an ethnic and anthropological range as wide, indeed somewhat wider, than Europe, and a federal structure which allows for great administrative autonomy, is nonetheless a clear unit. Its sources of instability are its religions, public corruption and the divergence in wealth between its people. By European standards India should fall apart. It may yet. There is no real pressure from inside for it to do so, however, except from those parts of the northern frontier which have always been uncomfortable with the Indian identity.

The European sense of communality, by contrast, has rarely extended beyond the conceptual, the geographic and the poetical. That it is possible to be a European has been recognized for several centuries. Until now, however, not much more has been expected of the idea than that it meant a shared railway network, a certain architectural heritage and the inheritance of Christianity. Even that religion, the defining characteristic of which was meant to be mutual respect and non-retaliation, has been used as one of the most potent forces of internal European destruction. The gift Europeans have for turning a mild disagreement over a matter of questionable importance into a solid reason for slaughter is astonishing.

The argument for continued conflict is easy to assemble. The nations of Europe, it asserts, have achieved their economic strength and their faith in themselves (which gives them a chauvinism able to withstand the verbal assaults of everybody else) by competing with a ferocity quite out of proportion to the resulting gain. When there has been nobody convenient to attack nearby, Europeans have looked as far away as they can reach. When the ends of the earth have been exhausted they have turned back against each other. Because this competitiveness has been so successful, without it Europe might collapse into self-indulgent irrelevance. Our history and our character demands that we cannot feel common interest even when we know it to be logical, as long as the price for pursuing it involves giving others a say in our affairs. So our only natural prospect for the future is to find a less murderous form of competition which allows all the perversity of national spirit while channelling the competitive drive into local enterprise. Only then will Europe be able to harness its energy – with each nation pursuing self-interest with independent vigour.

It is an attractive argument but it has too many holes to be worn with any comfort. The alternative offers a warmer vision and one which is no less appreciative of the differences which Europeans cherish so much more than their similarities. However, the forces that have made Europe see itself as less dominant than before are also those which make co-operation thinkable. These include the collapse of empires, humility in the aftermath of war, the opportunity given to the rest of the world by Europe's retreat from the global picture, the rise of the American and Far Eastern economies, the ease of travel, the salutary view of a complete world from space and the pervasiveness of American culture and the puritan values that go with it. It is a long list but by no means exhaustive. The size of the European market, now that Eastern and Western Europe are back together again in the same bloc, means that business has over 750 million people to sell to: still only the same as India but the largest developed consumer market outside China nonetheless. Whatever the gut feeling of Europe's people about the degree of trust they are prepared to place in each other, for politicians supported by business there is no other possibility than to make the single market a reality.

This has of course been recognized in all the instruments and treaties that have set up and developed the European Union. The

Single European Act, The Maastricht Treaty and its successors, will be seen in future decades as remarkably progressive and enlightened documents when their utilitarian origins are taken into account. The fact that they go beyond the necessities of trade and economic harmonization to a level of shared polity unknown in Europe since the Roman Empire is in itself a tribute to the vision of its driving personalities. That they recognize too that it is not enough for politicians to pool their decision-making powers, but that new continentally inclusive judicial and democratic structures need to complement the Council of Ministers also shows a maturity that Europe has encouraged abroad, but has not always been able to live up to at home. The insistence on democracy as the only acceptable form of government for the members of a club which almost all European states wish to join has delivered more freedom for the citizen in a quarter of a century than theoretical exhortation did in two hundred years. There can be little doubt that the determination not to be left out of shared relative prosperity was a crucial factor in the way Portugal, Greece, Spain and later Central and Eastern Europe shook off totalitarian regimes. The desire not to be beyond hope of inclusion continues to act as a discipline, sometimes effective, sometimes depressingly not, on Croatia, Turkey, Slovenia, Albania and Cyprus.

The social welfare traditions of the most caring countries are being spread to other societies with a record that is more libertarian. The arguments of the latter that increased entitlement automatically reduces competitiveness have not changed much since the start of the industrial revolution. Governments and traders were crying that minimum wages, controls on child labour and the introduction of copyright would bankrupt them all through the nineteenth century. What actually bankrupted them was their insistent belief that their imperial aims could be achieved by war with each other.

* * *

It is in the tradition of a social market, founded on democratic interdependence, that the project for the unification of all or most

17

of the European currencies has been put into operation. There are good economic arguments for a union of the myriad European currencies. There are equally good arguments against. One is that the diversity of currencies allows a flexibility in the trade between regions which reflects the different speed and conditions of their economic development. A single currency is terrific when everybody is doing equally well. When some or most are doing badly it makes prospects for the laggards worse while holding back the most successful. It is, though, more than an argument about effective economic frameworks. The fact that the debate has also widened to pit national pride against political ambition shows that the potential rifts in the enterprise are becoming uncomfortably visible.

The strains are multiple and their causes manifold: a mistrust of any 'big idea' imposed by a German Chancellor; mistrust of an inner circle of nations (basically the original six European Community members with the addition of Spain) by others who have different traditions (Nordic, Atlantic or Mediterranean); mistrust of nations states themselves by those whose regional allegiance is stronger than their loyalty to the member state of which they are part; mistrust of politicians who want to give up emotive totems of national identity like the mark and the franc; mistrust of unelected bankers having too much power in a democratic system; mistrust of businesses pushing through massive change for their own convenience (especially when the business are American, Japanese and Korean); mistrust of the blossoming influence of distant bureaucrats; and mistrust of experts who tell us that something revolutionary and potentially disastrous is all for our own good and that there is no alternative.

For those who see their own political time and capital running out and for whom the integration of the nations of Europe is the imperative of a lifetime's public service, such exhibitions of mistrust are more than annoying, they border on modern heresy. If there can be sedition in an open democratic society, those that preach against the goals of a united, though not necessarily unitary Europe, must be guilty of it. It is exasperating to see populations too lazy to turn out to vote for the European Parliament, to watch as referenda only just approve their carefully constructed treaties, to listen as respected former ministers and officials warn of social unrest as the consequence of monetary union.

It is tempting to load opprobrium on the cantankerous British – or more accurately the English – for standing in the way of progress, for being apologists for American interests, for being typical islanders and always wanting to be separate from the continental order. Britain is a convenient whipping boy, often unsubtle and undiplomatic in its criticism and strident in its demand for exclusivity. It is easy to distract the citizens of middle Europe by pointing to the late arrivals, the arrogant old imperialists whose suits are over formal and whose own institutions creak with age, people from across the sea who retain an aristocracy and do not even have a written constitution. Britain, by insisting that every line of every proposal is scrutinized and worried at as though it were an automatic removal of its fundamental rights, does not do much to help its case.

That is not the whole story, though. In every country in the Union and in many just outside, the engines of mistrust are turning over. Germans worry about the loss of the deutschmark and the authority of their regional governments. The Danish worry that they will be sucked south, dissolving the barrier with Germany which they have spent so long constructing. The French worry about their farming practices and the national destiny. The Belgians worry about their place in Brussels as it is over-run with European institutions, making them feel much as the citizens of Geneva do towards the United Nations. The Dutch do not take kindly to being told to toughen up their drugs laws by a French President of very different political persuasion from their own. Austrians do not want to share their country with anyone unless they are tourists.

Such fears reach beyond the confines of economic and political logic and convenience. Often they do not make any sense. Sometimes the sense they make is surely too ephemeral to dislodge the great project of European cohesion from its course. This is the view taken by those who believe that a technocratic view is sufficient, that governments can and do set policies and stick to them. They may well be right and order may triumph to produce a tidy and agreeable continent.

If they are wrong however, then either monetary union, the European Union itself and the project of reconciliation between east and west will fail; or another way, using another analysis, must be found to provide the direction. All the arguments confronting the unifiers have but two sources: the first is a feeling that the promises of a better life which union offers cannot be kept; the second is a terror that union will take away peoples' sense of belonging, the elements of their culture that define themselves and give them identity in a world where unemployment, mass communications and distant government are all doing their best to make identity undervalued and insecure. It is a cultural problem and it must therefore have cultural solutions. That is what the following chapters will examine and try to provide.

II
Perspectives

Then cam' fae east and west i' pride
    An' some cam sailan owre the sea,
An' a' tae win her for a bride;
    But never a bride wad the lady be.

George Mackay Brown,
An Orkney Tapestry

Outside the front door of my mother's house in Shetland there is a mound of earth. From the porch it is barely visible as the land slopes away to the bog at the bottom of the field and then on for a mile or so to the sea. Behind the house, a little above and even more exposed to the south-westerly gales, lie the ruins of the old house, one room with a substantial oven and small windows angled to frustrate the wind. The roof would have been of peat turves or sheaves of reeds weighted down by stones, heavy and pungent but as good an insulation as any modern fibreglass. It is almost impossible to date this ruin accurately, though the chimney suggests that it cannot have been much earlier than the seventeenth century. We know when it was abandoned though, because about 1820 a ship foundered on the vicious rocks that line the western coast of Shetland's Mainland and the contents of the ship's cash box salvaged from the wreck were enough to let the farmer move from the tiny croft into a proper house: two storeys, four rooms, windows with glass and a garden with a wall just high enough to stave off the blown salt and so let a few vegetables flourish in the short summer.

The new builder did not try to be too original. The house was lined up with the doorway looking south, across to the small island of Vaila, just as it had in the croft. But the croft builder himself

21

had been following an earlier model, though it is doubtful whether he knew it. The mound a few yards down the hill had the same perspective, the best position and a design far better at defeating the wind than either of its modern rivals. It was also a croft or small farmhouse, built to sleep five or six in alcoves around the walls. The door was protected by an elegant porch which curved round against the prevailing wind so that the house had the shape of an inverted comma. This house, so elegant and satisfying in shape and position, was built sometime in the middle bronze age, between 1500 and 500 BC, which makes it contemporary either with the Trojan War or the beginnings of the Athenian state. Shetland was warmer then, the grass richer and its population of sheep farmers was larger than it is now but the view was just the same. Because there are almost no trees in Shetland – the blown salt sees to that – there has been nothing but old grass to hide the site. So outside its front door are piles of small stones, discarded neatly from the cooking pot in which they were dropped as immersion heaters to keep the mutton stew bubbling. There has been no pressing need to disturb them in the three thousand years since they were tossed away.

This corner of Europe's far north west may not have the romance or the architectural glory of Delphi or Cordova but in a quiet and perhaps more satisfying way it illustrates the continuity of life in these lands. We have no real idea who the farmers were who made such fine round houses; early Celts, perhaps, of the British speaking race that a few hundred years later were known to the Romans (who met but could not defeat them) as Picts. More likely they were predecessors of the Celts, conceivably related to one of only two groups of Europeans still having a toehold on the continent from that time, the Finno-Ugrians or Basques. But I doubt it. One can draw hope instead from a much simpler fact that does not need historical speculation to affirm. Over the course of three millennia those who settled Shetland all came to the same conclusion about the best way to live on the same piece of land; about where was the most pleasant place to sit out in the sun and gaze out to sea; about the right size for a house that had to depend on a peat fire for its heating in the wet but chilly northern winter; about the right spot to keep an eye on the sheep without too much effort. We are not so very different from each other when the cosmetics of time and habits are stripped away. In that has lain the strength of Europe but also its perennial weakness.

From 500 BC until 2000 AD four peoples and many rulers have occupied Shetland. There was the Bronze Age builder, maybe a descendent of one of those that slashed and burnt the forests in the way they still do in Brazil, until the warm many-species woodland, home to boar and deer, had nothing to protect it against the salty wind and was only fit for sheep and ponies not much bigger. After him the Iron Age Pict, leaving only a few traces of runic script, a temple or two and some wonderfully decorated stones surviving from a culture that, like the Etruscan and Minoan, was so threatening to its conquerors that no written or linguistic shard was allowed to remain except in the names of hills and rivers (though the Picts, being Celts, may have followed the druidic prohibition on writing in their own tongue and been expunged before literate Christianity could preserve the evidence). Whether the Picts in Shetland were vanquished by the Scots, sweeping over from Hibernia and up from their new southern kingdom of Dalriada before the Vikings invaded from the east is hard to know for certain. If the Scots did conquer then, in the eighth century AD, it was not for long. The Norsemen felt at home in Shetland. It is, after all, nearer Bergen than Aberdeen (a name which is close to modern Welsh and so may itself be a Pictish survivor). They remained there long after the islands to the south had been over-run by Saxons and Normans, ceding Shetland to Scotland as part of a marriage dowry in 1469. In many senses they remain there still. *Up-helly-aa* is the Shetland Norse festival of winter fire, celebrated each January with the burning on the beach of a new longboat. The Shetland dialect has a dictionary full of Scandinavian words and Foula, the solitary island twenty miles off the coast from my mother's window, still claims to have a few people left who can converse in old Norse.

Now Scotland rules Shetland and England rules Scotland and Europe rules England. And Shetland has the oil which fuels them all. It is a circle which is not without humour. The most forgotten and sparsely populated land in Europe now sits on Europe's most precious asset and has, as a result, more airports per head of the population than anywhere else (five for twenty-five thousand). Ask who lives in Shetland now and the answer is that it reflects its true status, a hybrid place which knows its history and knows too that no single national ruler stays for very long.

Shetland never seems to have been a place for violent invasions. People have come, settled and assimilated without the need for killing on any scale. The castles, two or three, are half-hearted affairs, cold, cheerless and with the fortifications untested except by the weather. From Shetland it is easier to see Europe in perspective.

The view of the continent seems just as turbulent as the inter-vening sea. Just as calm at times, too. The way Europe has been populated in the years since the Bronze Age house was aban-doned has some of the sea's rhythm and some of its contradictions. As waves of invaders have pushed forward, so they have occupied the land, lying in still pools as though they had been there for ever, until the next wave comes and obliterates without memory or compunction.

It is a cruel rhythm and it means that no nation or nationality in Europe has unbloodied hands. We have behaved badly not only to those we have colonized overseas but as badly, possibly worse, to one another. If Europeans share anything it is a pattern of aggression. From the Celtic raids on the Etruscans in the fourth century BC to the German expansion of the third Reich the game of murder and sequestration has been the same. Sometimes the attacks have been armed robbery on a grand scale, sometimes they have been full blown conquest, sometimes the obliteration of a class or race. In the twentieth century Nazi Germany attemp-ted all three at once. More recently the Serbs and Croats have been developing a new variant of the recipe with the first two ingredients subordinate to the third.

After these periodic but depressingly regular bouts of blood-letting the political map seems to settle down into its new arrangements relatively quickly. Borders are redrawn, envoys exchanged and accredited, trade routes and local industry re-established. For a time all seems quiet and surprisingly peaceful. It is easy for the conquerors to believe after a few years, a generation or two, that their position is inalienable and, more dangerously, quite natural.

It is simple to see how this happens. As the landscape recovers (whether urban or rural) it is easy to forget without conscious effort that it was ever different. Humans adapt to new surroundings extremely fast, at least for the purposes of everyday activity. They also only usually attack one another when they are convinced that they will be in danger or will lose materially if they do not. More often than not acquisition of other people's land and goods is justified either by citing the threat that they pose or by asserting that they have no rights to them in the first place. The excuses boil down to four classic justifications; 'they've got plenty more where that came from', 'the way they got it was no better than how we did', 'if we didn't take it someone else would', and 'we did it to them before they did it to us'.

The last is the most potent. The one guaranteed way for leaders – a loose term given the self-interested thugs they usually are – to rouse their followers sufficiently so that they perpetrate appalling violence on those living nearby, is by convincing them that they themselves are about to be slaughtered or driven from their land. Most European people are from farming roots, however urban they may have become later, so there is therefore no more effective call to action than the threat of being driven from the land. When this is allied with the doctrine that the best form of defence is attack and bolstered by stories of past atrocity (aimed at the society's reproductive system, the women and children, and therefore doubly emotive), there is rarely any difficulty in galvanising groups to behave quite outside their normal character.

Every nation and sub-nation in Europe has behaved in this way at some time in the last three thousand years. There is no-one who can legitimately claim to have arrived in the first instance by agreed settlement. This is not the same as saying that every individual has acquired territory by force., which is obviously not the case. However the national or ethnic group from which each person comes has almost always arrived in the vicinity through invasion rather than gradual inter-marriage and commercial arrangement. It is a view over which archaeologists and anthropologists argue strongly. It is clearly not enough to assume that every hectare of land has been taken from former owners by force. But equally the sudden arrival of large groups in an area could not be accomplished by peaceful means. The Barbarian, Frankish, Saxon, Viking, Mongol and Celtic hordes were very real and uncompromisingly violent, as were the Romans, the Huns, the Persians and the Ottomans and Seljuk Turks.

Between these great invasive waves there were plenty of confrontations to fill the gaps. Tribal and clan warfare has been just as effective in keeping Europe violent as the full scale ethnic attack. From the families of Sicily and the Mafia they have perpetuated to the clans of Sinclairs, Gunns and Mackays in Caithness, in the northernmost corner of Scotland, the rivalry has been bloody and abiding.

The latter is particularly instructive because the three clans, all lumped together now as Scottish, reflect both the sequence and the means by which power has been shifted between ethnic groups. In Britain's usefully (for this purpose) anachronistic class system the distinctions are clear even today. Telling the story backwards, the Earl of Caithness was a Minister in John Major's Government, the late Viscount Thurso was a leading member of the Liberal Democrat party. Both families are Sinclairs and, like the Gordons who dominate the lands to the south and west as Dukes of Sutherland, the Sinclairs are Norman in origin, arriving in Britain from the middle of the eleventh century and fighting their way north. The Sinclairs still form the majority of the middle or professional classes indigenous to the area.

Lord Reay was also a Minister in John Major's Government and has served as a member of the European Parliament and a delegate to the Council of Europe. His ancestors, banished from Strathnaver (the country immediately to the west of Caithness) through the machination of the Gordon Dukes of Sutherland, included an influential commander in the Danish forces during the Thirty Years War and others who, a generation later, were in the service of the Dutch Princes (from which time the present Lord Reay holds a Barony in the Netherlands). Lord Reay holds a less senior aristocratic title than the three Norman lords that are his neighbours, a hereditary barony, the lowest title which, at the time of writing, allows a family a continuous seat in the House of Lords, the Upper House of the British Parliament. As Dukes, Earls and Viscounts, the Lords of Sutherland, Caithness and Thurso have no more voting power than Lord Reay but their sons are given honorary lordships while their fathers are still alive and it is assumed, rightly, that their inherited lands are more extensive. At any State occasion they would have precedence over an 'ordinary' Baron.

Lord Reay is a Mackay. The Mackays are Gaels, true Scots, or as their Norman neighbours and the Stuart Kings referred to them up until the beginning of the nineteenth century, 'barbarous Irish' who had spread to the far north by the middle of the tenth century. Generally in northern Scotland the social position of Mackays is still less prosperous than that of the Norman Sinclairs.

The Gunns, the third clan, are most commonly settled in the small villages and depressed towns on the barren coast of Caithness. They seem to be the oldest of the three families to live there, tracing their lineage back to the Vikings who established the 'earldom' of Orkney in the ninth century. They have no stake in the ruling houses of modern Britain (though Gunns have served it well as soldiers, diplomats, businessmen and poets) and at home Gunns were looked down upon in local Highland society. The expectations of Gunns are still thought to be lower and there is a feeling, even among the schoolchildren of modern Caithness, that the Gunns as a clan are not in the same league as the Mackays, let alone the Sinclairs.

The relative progress of these three families is matched in similar situations in hundreds of places throughout Europe. The sequence of ethnic invasion determines the social status for generations after the invaders have been theoretically fully assimilated into the host country. All three families boast tartans, the badge of Celtic Scotland. All three would also claim to be utterly British, even though strictly the term British was revived only in the early years of the eighteenth century after the governmental union between England and Scotland. It was expropriated from the original pre-Roman inhabitants of the islands with which the Vikings, Gaels and Normans have no connection. Yet despite the passage of centuries and the contribution of individual clan members to every aspect of national and imperial life, the basic hierarchy of invasion remains substantially intact. The Vikings giving way to the Gaels (in a reversal of the process happening on the east coast of Ireland at the same time) who in turn were subjugated by the Norman French Stuart Kings of Scotland and their Hanoverian successors, a process not completed until after the Highland clearances in the middle of the nineteenth century.

Given that there was only a century or so between each ethnic arrival, the survival of the hierarchy – often unconscious, sometimes very conscious indeed – for a further thousand years suggests that there is a vital connection between daily politics and the folk memory of settlement. Our assumptions about those we deal with in business, in official and personal life, are influenced by a series of perceptions which reach back much further than is credited. We are programmed by an array of influences which are normally kept in check. However when we feel our way of life, our prosperity or our sense of place to be under threat, we fall back on these influences as the base on which we try to build new security. Our fundamental perspectives are much longer than we realize. They are many hundreds of years longer than journalists or economists acknowledge when they search in bafflement for reasons why conflict flares over issues which to outsiders are trivial and could be resolved with relative ease.

I have used examples from Shetland and northern Scotland not just because I know them well but because for most mainland Europeans they are places sufficiently exotic, even romantic, not to cause offence when the curiosities are pointed out. However France is certainly not immune from such distinctions. Neither is Spain, Italy or Austria and most Germans can soon work out where someone comes from, and at what social level, by looking at the name. In a complicated society this is not surprising. Only in one with a shorter immigrant history and one where current prosperity defines social influence – as in the United States or Australia (though there too the distinction of being descended from the indigenous pre-colonial population risks serious discrimination, even if it is now more attitudinal than legal) – are lineage and family longevity not quickly apparent. One would find the same attention to detail in India, Indonesia or South Africa.

However, if the hangover of ancient family or clan power play is of interest to sociologists but not of over-riding importance in a wider context, when the folk memory reaches out to colour entire regions or ethnic groups the effect is far more significant. Folk memory is not the same as history, though it may contain surprisingly accurate elements carried down the centuries as near myth which then turn out to be well supported by archaeology. Folk memory conflates and dismembers stories, allocating incidents to culprits and heroes who are in reality many years away from the true perpetrators. It gives motives and significance to known historical figures which utterly misrepresent their reasons for action. Most of all it shortens and lengthens perspectives so that it banishes quite recent occurrence, like the founding of nationhood, to a time so far distant that the rights and emotions derived from it are unquestionable; lost in beliefs about natural evolution or quasi-religion. Simultaneously, though, folk memory promotes ancient grievances to a position far nearer in the historical record so that actions which were rooted firmly in the politics of their own day are endowed with a patina of justification or condemnation from much further back.

The great advantage of folk memory is that it does not have to be proved by documentary or archaeological evidence. The anecdote, even the feeling in the gut, is enough. To take another British example, according to many the reason why the Labour Party, despite its more popular policies and the unpopularity of the tired conservative government, failed to win the 1992 general election was because it was led by Neil Kinnock, a man who was recognized as competent and often inspiring but who was and sounded Welsh. The folk memory that the English can never trust the Welsh, which goes back to the traumatic time English settlers had in Wales after it was conquered in 1282 and the uprising of Owain Glyn Dŵr a century later, meant that just too many English voters could not bring themselves to vote for a Welshman as Prime Minister.

This can be seen as unreasonable prejudice causing individual tragedy for an able man. But it also carries with it the thought that relations between the largest member states in the European Union during the years following his defeat would have been very different if the man who went on to become a Commissioner had instead been allowed to lead his country. It is not the first time it has happened. The same reason may have been behind Lloyd George's inability to win an election except as part of a coalition. So the Liberal who had paved the way for the modern welfare state, ensured a generous armistice settlement in 1918 and changed England's policy of repression towards Ireland, was removed at a crucial moment in Britain's social development and that of his own party.

Other countries have similar fears about the origins and therefore the dependability of leaders if they do not come from the metropolitan elite, clustered at the centre of the dominant ethnic power. For many in France there was always a nagging doubt about Napoleon, not just because he was a megalomaniac but because he was Corsican. Equally, had King Constantine of Greece been naturally Greek rather than demonstrably German it is likely that he would have regained the throne in the 1970s after the collapse of the Colonels' regime in the same way that Juan Carlos of Spain did after the death of Franco.

These are personal cases where 'deviant' nationality – deviating from that acknowledged by the great mass of the population – has a lasting and profound political effect. These issues rarely surface openly because it is normally too impolite to refer to them: even arrogant nations have a vestige of conscience about discrimination. However when they are applied beyond the personal to the general they feed two processes; the mythology of nationalism and the definition of culture.

As might be expected from the Scottish examples discussed above, the virulence of national feeling is often in inverse ratio to the age of national settlement. Because it has had such a strong recent political and emotional effect, with the breaking up of Czechoslovakia into Slovakia and the cumbersomely named Czech Republic, the progress of Czech nationalism is worth taking some space to examine. The Velvet revolution of 1989 which freed the country from the Soviet Empire and saw the elevation to President of Vaclav Havel, one of the continent's most perceptive and, in the best senses of the word, civilized writers, at first seemed to be cementing the achievement of the dream of independence recognized in 1918. The Soviet-backed regime had always realized that there were strains between the two halves of a long country – its western half more closely identified with Germany and Austria, its eastern half nearer in allegiance to Bulgaria, Poland and the Ukraine – and had placed an internal border between Brno and Bratislava. Now that border has become an external one between two separate European nations following very different routes of political and economic development, even though the actual history of the region prior to the First World War would argue for central European consolidation into some sort of post Austro-Hungarian confederation, instead of the complicated patchwork of small states which now demand acceptance.

The reality of Czech nationalism is rather different from the legend fostered at the end of the nineteenth century and given emotional charge by the glorious operas of Smetana and the nationalistic symphonic poems of Dvorak and Suk. Slavs entered the area in large numbers in the fifth century, not always displacing but certainly putting pressure on the Germanic and the remnants of the Celtic population already there. Along with the similar arrivals further north of Poles and Balts it was probably one of the causes of the knock-on effect which made the previously containable Franks and Norse move west so aggressively themselves.

The eastern part of the country, modern Slovakia, drew its racial influences from the east and south (Ukraine and Hungary) while the west adopted the Slavic language of the new arrivals but otherwise drew much of its cultural references – alphabet, architecture, drinking habits, food and feudal system – from the Germanic world into which it had penetrated. This area then redefined itself again as Bohemia and Moravia, with Slovakia developing a separate linguistic identity that went further than being a dialect only as late as the nineteenth century. Gradually over the last two hundred years the population has become more homogenous, with political upheavals since the establishment of the Czechoslovak state in 1918 leading to a forced exodus of most of the remaining German population (thus completing the invasion attempted but not fully achieved 1500 years before) and a more peaceful but no less drastic removal of Hungarians and Ukrainians. As a result the largest remaining non-Slav minority in the area are the Gypsies, the treatment of whom by all countries still illustrates the extraordinary fear that Europeans have towards any ethnic group that does not share its agrarian or urban living patterns or which questions the legitimacy of territorial nationalism. It is a lesson Europe's Jews have learnt to their intense cost too, of course. Unless a culture and an ethnic group can be identified with a territory they will rarely be tolerated for any length of time, especially if the host nationality is either under threat or is seeking to extend itself. Europe's new ethnic minorities – Asian, African and Caribbean – are discovering the continuing accuracy of this assertion.

For all the passion attached to it, though, the legitimacy of nationalism is thoroughly suspect. The boundaries that seem so absolute, whereby crossing an imaginary line, often without any topographical logic, sees an immediate change in language, law and living patterns, is both artificial and recent. This does not make it any less effective. Charlemagne's old capital, the centre of the last relatively civilized attempt to unite the Germanic peoples (this deliberately excludes the Nazis as uncivilized, barbarians as Rome in its fearful last years would have understood the term) is either Aachen or Aix-la-Chappelle depending on which tradition is followed. It lies in an area which for centuries changed its allegiance from east to west according to the balance of power. One might expect that, like Luxembourg, its duality would be apparent still. Now, however, it is as emphatically German as it is possible to imagine. A taxi driver crossing the border into Walloon Belgium only a few kilometres away is immediately lost, linguistically and geographically. A short journey, no further, to the north takes him into Dutch Limburg with the same result.

Much the same attitude can be found even in Alsace, its capital Strasbourg recognising its ambiguous identity by serving as the centre for modern European efforts to behave itself, where France has ensured that Alsatian is rarely heard and that there is no evidence of it in visible printed material. Equally France and Germany ensure that the Rhine remains a rigorous divider of the two modern states which at other political and economic levels are trying to construct a new European order on the back of their alliance.

No nation sees itself as aggressive or naturally war-like. In reality the very act of national declaration is a matter of asserting difference from others living nearby and is bound to be aggressive in some measure, though it does not have to be a matter of physical assault. It can be a legal framework which is discriminatory – the fact that European states still require each other's citizens to register as 'aliens', the same word as one would use for a being with three heads from the far end of the galaxy, is instructive. It can just be the coldness with which people greet each other or a reluctance to ask neighbours into the home.

Usually the more abused the nation feels itself to be, the more virulently it tries to assert its individuality and territorial hegemony. This is classically illustrated in the way the newly independent Baltic states are behaving towards the ethnic Russians who have in fact demonstrated their belief in and loyalty to the new country, in which most of them have lived all their lives, by choosing to stay. For those that feel that they have a racial right to the territory, the willingness of outsiders to co-operate and join together in the process of economic and political development is irrelevant. At any moment in European history the trappings of national identity can seem only to be as safe as the state with which they are most associated.

Because it is so precarious, nationalism is invoked with disproportionate passion. There is a good reason for this as well as a bad one. For all of its history Europe has been aching for some stability which did not involve being conquered by someone else, whether that someone was a tribal invader, Napoleon, the Swedes, the Kaiser or Hitler. A non-aggressive sense of national worth gives an illusion of security, which is especially important for a group of people for whom the principle driving force has always been tenure of the land. That security cannot come from legal documents alone, even when there is agreement about their validity beyond the borders of the issuing state. It has to be fortified with a personal and local social surety; the knowledge that one holds the land or belongs in a community by right which cannot be removed. The fact that it is all too easy to remove not only the right but the holder lies at the base of the insecurity. It would be nice to think that the reason why Europeans feel so unsure of their ability to sustain their tenure is because they realize that they themselves have all been agents of seizure only a few generations in the past and feel guilty about it. Humanity does not seem to work like that, however. The most certain nations, the most vociferous that they have an automatic right to the land they occupy and that their society represents as closely as possible the natural order, are those with the most recent history of violent settlement. Israel is a striking example of this. In a later chapter it will be the aim of this book to discuss how Europe can maintain a sense of individual and group security while simultaneously matching the aspirations of an interdependent and sophisticated society.

The necessary conclusion that most national mythology is just illegitimate history given substance by emotional need, does not make it any less relevant to the debate about how to reshape the role of states in an intercontinental economic climate; one that was largely created by European expansion and was fashioned in its own image but which has now broken free from its inventor's control. Nationalism is still the most powerful force in European political psychology and a version of it underpins all the structures which have been put together to supersede it. The realization that this is indeed the long term intention is the cause of the intemperate rancour that flows just under the level of diplomacy and government.

Those that think the European Union is a machine for transferring national decision making from local parliaments to a supra-national bureaucracy inadequately supervised by a continental parliament based in Brussels are wrong. This may well be the effect but it is not the intention. The concept of pooled sovereignty is actually a desperate attempt to enable nineteenth-century Bismarckian and Third Empire nationalism to succeed after the disaster of three wars across the Rhine in a hundred years. France and Germany have realized that, despite disparities in population size and economic performance, they are effectively evenly matched. Open hostilities between them therefore only have the effect of cancelling both out as world powers and enervating the rest of the continent, which cannot avoid being drawn into their conflicts (though Spain and Britain have sufficient geographical independence and transatlantic alliances to remain aloof for a comparatively short time). While Germany was disunited, or rather while its potential was split between Prussia and the Austro-Hungarian Empire with a collection of dependent but autonomous states acting as a buffer on the eastern side of the Rhine, it was possible for Germany and France to contain their conflicts. France did not do so, of course, always seeing the German states close by as having the potential of widening the Frankish empire back to Carolingian proportions. The Hapsburgs hankered after Charles V's abdicated central power and Prussia, Denmark and Sweden vied for control of the north. The Thirty Years War, the War of Spanish Succession (which still resonates in the dispute between Britain and Spain over Gibraltar, a miserable piece of rock with a suburban ethos which would shame any decent Spanish town) and the campaigns of Louis XIV and Napoleon were the result.

With the Rhine becoming the principle border between major unified powers however, a modus vivendi had to be reached. Three times united Germany tried French invasion tactics and the outcome was the same as it had been for France: after initial success Germany lost with disastrous consequences. Chancellor Kohl's assertion that the only alternative to European integration has to be war is based upon this experience. The only way for France and Germany to pursue their national ambitions, the significance which they believe their potential strength and character entitles them to, is to form a joint empire in which the machinery allows others to participate but which essentially concentrates administrative decision-making along the geographical line of their division; from Basle to the sea – Frankfurt, Strasbourg and Brussels. Frankfurt's name (the ford of the Franks) is beginning to sound thoroughly appropriate. There is a positive and less sinister motive too, of course. It would be distorting the truth to suggest that France and Germany did not also believe in the positive benefits of a peaceful and integrated Europe that does more than just hold the line down the middle of the Rhine. All the liberal measures brought about by the Maastricht treaty – freedom of movement and trade, joint decision-making, military and civil co-operation – are evidence of the urge to invent a new humanist structure for government that secures everybody's standard of living. As long as this arrangement really does keep France and Germany in balance, with each being able to claim a measure of leadership and the common market thus created delivering rising living standards and foreign esteem to the population, then Kohl's project (which he has sold so hard to two French Presidents) is likely to be successful.

However there can be no doubt that a twin-headed empire is in the making as a result, though it is not yet despotic and, if democratic checks and balances are strengthened, may never grow to be so. The other original members of the European Community, Italy and the Benelux, will have little option but to follow the Franco-German lead. Along with Austria their own chances of matching the prosperity of the joint power-base depend on it. Spain realizes its potential for separate development is limited without its Latin American empire; the painful lesson of the Franco years has been well digested. Italy, fought over by its northern and western neighbours for a millennium and a half, wants the political respect its culture has always enjoyed. Portugal and Ireland have historical reasons for distrusting their immediate neighbours and prefer to hitch themselves to other wagons a little further away, especially when considerable sums of money are being delivered with the invitation. They, like the Benelux, cannot seriously affect the basic policies but they can ensure a measure of national attention in the polite machinery of EU diplomacy which they could never hope to merit on their own. They are useful subordinates, able to chair contentious meetings and offer a semblance of real partnership in return for an occasional place in the limelight.

The European Union has developed further than this, however, on the back of idealism rather than hard political advantage. The rhetoric that accompanies the project argues that all Europe must seek to be united, that there is a common cultural heritage and a convergence of interest that should make the Union a source of consummate brotherhood; a political manifestation of Schiller's Ode to Joy (*An die Freude*) which in Beethoven's setting has been adopted as the anthem. It is a noble ideal, the counterpart to the violent and self-interested aims of the Germanic peoples which this chapter has chronicled up to now. Moreover it is rhetoric backed by commendable logic. It calls for the nations of Europe to equal North America, China and the ASEAN states in a way which the dissipated fallen empires of the continent can never hope to do again. More importantly its emphasis on democracy, objective financial management, equal rights, social protection and interlocking institutions is put forward as the guarantee of a lasting peace, the like of which western Europe has not enjoyed since the second century AD.

These are benefits which are too attractive to be ignored and so Sweden and Finland have followed Denmark, Greece and Britain into the Union while many others, which already participate at the trade level via the European Free Trade Association (EFTA) and on the cultural, human rights and democracy level via the Council of Europe, seek to join, hoping to cement their national standing through admission to what they see as the club of winners. Turkey, both parts of Cyprus, the Czech Republic, Poland, Hungary, Slovakia, Slovenia and the three remaining small Baltic states now clamour to be allowed in.

Only Norway has decided that, having tasted life inside the Community (as the venture was entitled until the ratification of the 1992 Treaty of Maastricht), it does not want to be part of the post-Maastricht Union. Norway's reservations led it to reject continued membership of the Union and for several others which had already joined and remained after Maastricht, similar reservations are now resulting in severe internal national divisions. These divisions are useful warnings to those hovering outside the circle of membership. In Denmark and Britain the strains on the political fabric caused by deeply held anxieties about national autonomy and influence are becoming hard to contain. For these states and potentially several others the advantages of joining the institutions of European union are only valuable as long as they deliver advantages in economic performance. For many of their citizens there is also advantage to be gained individually from the opportunities to participate in activities which have a wider perspective than that of their own national boundaries.

However, although all these countries were enormously

affected by involvement in the 1914-18 and the 1939-45 wars –
in Britain's case accelerating its political and economic decline in
world rankings by several decades – the fundamental worries
over cross-Rhine aggression are only tangential in actual peace-
time. So long as Germany and France are in harmony they are a
very different threat from when they are at war. England's foreign
policy since the beginning of the sixteenth century has been
shaped by its island position and its natural inclination to seek
the central ground, keeping the balance between the other two,
slightly larger, Germanic powers and stopping either one
becoming too dominant. Scotland, inherently suspicious of any
policy emanating from the southern half of the island, has
traditionally favoured France – thus balancing another sub-plot;
the potential alliance between England and the petty princes of
the Netherlands and the pre-Bismarck German States. In the
contemporary version of the game, while English nationalists
regard the concept of Europe itself as a threat, the nationalists in
Scotland and Wales see it as the first opportunity in three hundred
years to join an entity that does not have London as its capital.

The danger inherent in the division between the core countries
and those on the periphery is that those which have a pragmatic
but not emotional reason to be enthusiastic supporters of union
will always carry substantial groups antagonistic to the idea as
part of their mainstream politics. This is true in all the Nordic
states and Britain. In fact most opinion poll evidence suggests
that popular support for European cohesion and much of the
institutional framework is strong but so is support for national
identity and independence. The division splits the electorate in
half. The difference between the original group of Community
countries and the new arrivals, however, is that in the first Treaty
of Rome a nation's opposition to the institutional framework of
Europe is excluded from mainstream politics. This does not mean
that it is any less prevalent in the electorate. It just means that it
is a taboo subject in political circles. The trouble with this is that
it casts any country which has reservations about the evolving
European machinery as, at best, backward and half-hearted, at
worst, traitors who threaten the peace.

Germany's constant assertion that the only alternative to the

Union is the breakdown of peace begins, in turn, to sound just as threatening to those whose social climate and reasons for joining are different. Yet there is no doubt that without this threat, the momentum towards integration would be slowed. Indeed two other scenarios could develop which the main German political parties would find difficult to absorb. In one, France would re-assert its wish to be the leader of the project, and in the other opponents, not of union itself, but of the dilution of German national identity would slow integration and demand more emphasis on domestic affairs. Many of the *länder* are already anxious to do this, fearful that their traditional autonomy is being sold on like a betting slip by the federal government.

By retaining the fiction that slower integration threatens peace, however, France and Germany are effectively ensuring that every criticism, however detailed, is portrayed as a failed test of loyalty. Ironically they are adopting Margaret Thatcher's old question of 'is he one of us?'. Either a country is with the Franco-German scheme or it is against it. The middle way is not encouraged and while this may make certain that the inner core of the union holds together whatever the social pressures, it may also guarantee that more disenchanted countries follow Norway's lead with great damage to themselves and to Europe's credibility as a continent able to demonstrate political maturity.

Whether or not faster integration makes economic or bureau-cratic sense – and in general it does – the leadership of the enterprize is moving much faster than the electorate. In a demo-cratic system there has to be a fine balance between just doing what the electorate seems to think it wants – which is doing without leadership at all – and being seen to have a leadership agenda which is so far in advance of the common sense that it runs the risk of looking like corporate dictatorship. An integrated Europe would be an administratively tidy Europe, though not necessarily administratively simple, and it would have fierce penalties for those (countries, companies or individuals) who littered the continent with untidy and inconvenient problems. As in even the most carefully regulated home, however, there will soon be muddy footsteps on the floor and dirty hand marks on the fresh paint. It is the lot of the politician and the bureaucrat that events always spoil the neatest of plans and the application forms always leave out the one crucial piece of information that would prevent disaster.

By this stage of the chapter there may well be readers who are convinced that I am arguing the sceptical case against European union; that I am failing the loyalty test and aligning myself with the raucous English and Danish nationalists. This is far from accurate. It is true to say, however, that there is a massive deficit in perceived support for most of the manifestations of the Union. The low turnout for elections to the European Parliament (even where voting is compulsory) and the close votes in the referenda on the Treaty of Maastricht are clear indications that real belief is lacking. Despite the fact that the institutions of Europe are in general far more open and liberal than national governments, and despite the huge amounts of money spent on trying to make information available and friendly, apathy and antipathy are spread broad and deep.

It is too easy to blame this on a failure of communication or on the stubbornness of national self-interest. Somewhere there is a vital element missing which is undermining the whole enlightened process. The empirical reasons for a harmonious and, at least in a loose sense, a federated Europe are well under-stood and broadly supported. Nonetheless while the minds judge in favour, many hearts are unconvinced. The missing element, rather like a quark in particle physics, is theoretically discovered but hard to measure. It has two descriptions which at the moment are in opposition to each other but which must be brought together if they are not to become mutually destructive; European consciousness and cultural allegiance.

III

Allegiances

A nation is a society united by a delusion about its ancestry and by a common hatred of its neighbours.

William Ralph Inge,
A Perpetual Pessimist

Generations of schoolchildren have first consciously identified their sense of place by writing out their address, in its longest possible form, on the cover of their exercise books. If one had been born in a suburb of Munich the inscription might have read something like this:–

> Hans Friedrich Schmidt,
> Apartment 7,
> Cardinalstr. 24,
> Giesing,
> Munich,
> Bavaria,
> Germany,
> Europe,
> The World,
> The Solar System,
> The Galaxy,
> The Universe.

Perhaps the only thing that has changed in my lifetime is that now one might have to specify which galaxy in which universe. For the future adult it is more than a place to send the post to; it is a list of allegiances which runs in reverse order of importance. Surprisingly, given the ease of travel and the supposed mobility of labour, comparatively few people venture far from their home ground except for holidays and business meetings. Even higher education, which is meant to broaden the mind, is usually delivered close to home. So the list contains the makings of a set of political assumptions and loyalties that will condition the individual throughout his or her career. Even if they are jolted by major disruptions – war, emigration, marriage to a foreigner, job postings to other countries – these political assumptions and loyalties are likely to be modified with experience but not substantially removed. To an extent only comprehensible in a society where territory and language go together, in Europe a remarkable amount of information that a person will use to draw conclusions and make decisions can be calibrated by knowing precisely where he or she comes from. Race, lineage, profession, class and income bracket are all vital components as well but geographical roots can often override them all.

The closer the observer is to someone's own experience, the more information can be gleaned from accent, dress, the house's position in the street and the reputation of the local school. A shared contact anywhere along the line will draw sympathy, though some points will be more potent than others. It is this hierarchy of allegiances which determines both the opportunities and the barriers that Europe faces in trying to build itself not just a co-operative future but a coherent one.

Because the European Union is essentially an intergovernmental concept, its allegiances are primarily towards the member states. This is reflected in the vesting of ultimate power in the Council of Ministers. In almost all cases (Sweden and the Netherlands being almost the only exceptions) these member states have existed in their present constitutional form for less than two hundred and fifty years, but as was discussed in Chapter II, emotional historical perspectives are much longer than that. Therefore when disagreement surfaces at a European level it is assumed by those whose natural forum is the member states that it is their interests, as defined in national terms, which will win the support and allegiance of the citizens. To an extent this is true; partly because it is understood that it is national power that is being relinquished in favour of European sovereignty, partly because the basic rule for the defence of allegiance is that one will be most vociferous about the tier of loyalty immediately below the one that is trying to expand its authority. So if the town is trying to knock down the street, one defends the street against the town. If the continent is being discriminated against in the motor trade, one defends Europe against Asia. Nation states therefore assume that they are the fundamental focus of allegiance, as they were in the past, whether that allegiance was expected to be expressed just for a nation or whether it was extended to an empire via an imperial family.

Since the entire purpose of the European Union project is to protect against national interest becoming so inflamed that it destabilizes Europe itself, the notion of the defence of national interest is a tricky one. It ensures that at the heart of all the decision-making institutions of union there lies a contradiction and an inevitable source of conflict. The veto on grounds of national interest or the protection of national culture and heritage should, if Europe is working properly, be redundant. A well-ordered system would ensure that proposals were so beneficial to all states that it automatically fulfilled the national aspiration while advancing the European position. This rarely happens, of course. Because the social and economic tapestry of Europe has been sown at such different speeds and with such different designs, any action is bound to remove favour from one section by transferring it elsewhere. The source of conflict is the perception that those nations which are in agreement over action – usually those for whom the benefits are apparent – see themselves as taking action in the name and interests of Europe, while those opposing the action in defence of their national interest will be seen to be acting out of selfishness. Since the automatic reaction to this is for the country or countries in the minority to defend their defined interest against the others with redoubled vigour as a matter of national pride, the potential for disputes to multiply is only limited by the fact that for the most part every country is sooner or later in the minority on one issue or another, and therefore the bad tempers that inevitably result do not last with one member more than another for long enough to cause serious disruption.

There are three exceptions to the caveat, though: France, Britain and Germany. France simply will not implement any proposal which it perceives as being offensive to its esteem or harmful to its interests, whether it has signed a piece of paper on the subject or not. Britain's utilitarian view of the Union means that it is not enough for a proposal to be broadly beneficial or neutral in its effect to be supported. It must be demonstrably an improvement (not for the citizen but for the vested interests of the Treasury and occasionally for corporations too) on anything that could be achieved under national policy. When two out of three of these states agree a policy, it is likely that the policy action will be applied to all the rest. If France and Germany agree then it is also likely that Britain will seek a derogation. If it succeeds the others will try to circumvent the derogation by applying the same measures from another direction. If less powerful or smaller countries press for action it is rare that they will achieve it without the support of France and Germany. Britain, however, usually pursues its policy of semi-detachment, its traditional diplomatic game of placing itself on the periphery and acting as a magnet for other malcontents and of being a focus for galvanising opposition to either France or Germany or both. Recently, though, Britain has found itself out-played by France and Germany for, as long as they are acting together, it is too dangerous for countries which share their borders to oppose them. Britain has found itself fulfilling Churchill's role which he defined so accurately while he was encouraging the original concept of a European community. 'Britain', he said, 'is in Europe but not of it.'

The tension involved in trying to run a continental union based on pooled nationalism is not going to be alleviated in the short term. The expectations brought to inter-governmental discussions mean that acquiescence or wariness towards France and Germany will always dominate the atmosphere. But it is compounded by the fact that there is no European institution where members are elected or appointed on anything other than a national basis. It is surely impossible to develop a trans-European consciousness when at every level the individuals sent to work on it are mandated by nation states with very different agendas for their behaviour. Junior officials of the Commission sometimes leave their national baggage behind, mainly because their training has meant that since leaving school very little of their adult lives has been spent in their country of origin. Now that the children of the first generation of officials are nearing middle age there is a breed which is truly European, with allegiances more to the institutions that they think of as home than to any particular country or even the cities that host the institutions themselves – a characteristic which is in danger of causing serious social disquiet in Brussels and Strasbourg where, as with the United Nations in New York and Geneva, the international officials are seen as alien creatures welded onto city life, consuming services but not contributing any sense of commitment.

At the Commissioner level, however, the nationalism is only thinly veiled by a protocol of impartiality. The Commissioners are chosen nationally and appointed for the most part as a reward for past political favours, often as a consolation for a career at home which has not lived up to expectations: ex-leaders of national parties, ex-ministers forced out by blameless resignation, those who came second in the race for national premiership. When they get to Brussels they take on some of the cosmetics of international allegiance but their cabinets, their own appointees who advise and filter contact with other officials and who devise the approach to policy, are mostly brought from the home nation. However distinguished the supranational credentials of the Spanish Commissioner, his cabinet will be Spanish too. It is a rule which runs true even for Luxembourg, where one might have thought that the pool of potential talent was limited enough to open the system to at least a sprinkling of outsiders.

At the European Parliament, a body which cannot function without cross-party and trans-national consensus, the member states still dominate the system. Although the allegiance of each MEP is meant to switch to the European group which brings together national parties of vaguely similar views (with some fairly odd results in terms of political labels), the basic loyalty is firmly anchored to the party back home. Whatever their alliances members will vote with their group's national subdivision, even if this means voting against their own European super-party. Jacques Santer owes his post as President of the European Commission to the fact that the Spanish Socialists voted against their own side in the confirmation hearings when the centre and left were otherwise united in their opposition. Depending on political strength at home, parties, particularly those where the European group is poorly ideologically defined, switch Parliamentary groups in an attempt to gain advantage and influence.

The European Parliament is undoubtedly more international in outlook than its national equivalents – it could hardly be otherwise given the agenda of directives it is sent to consider – but in the two decades since it was directly elected for the first time it is still to the host nation that the members look for their job security. National parties draw up their lists and even though there has been a half-hearted attempt to put the name of the European group on some election literature, very few voters would be able to name the supra-national party for which they are voting. Because the power of patronage is firmly in the hands of local parties, so the calibre and principal interests of the members are coloured by the preoccupations of their national debate, They even behave quite differently at home than they do in Brussels and Strasbourg. Meet an Italian MEP at home and the attentive, reasonable international statesman turns into the traditional urbane but disingenuous local operator, quite incapable of giving the tolerably straight answer delivered happily a few days before in the European arena.

The election system ensures that members of the Parliament are permanently schizophrenic, their allegiances pulled by the concerns of the nation state. It is of course a limitation which has always dogged federal legislatures. The tradition of deal-making on local interests in the United States Congress has given rise to exactly the same conundrum of attempting to legislate on behalf of the whole of the federation while advancing the financial and social agendas of the representative's own home town or state. In one sense the European Parliament is a step ahead of that because of the list system so that members are not in theory identified with a particular locality. However this also means that they are wholly within the power of national parties, with no independent political base of their own and therefore no reason to adopt an individual or supranational position on any issue. Although there is considerable distrust between parliamentarians in national assemblies and those in the European one – with national members convinced that they are not in control and that their colleagues in Brussels are taking a damagingly independent line – the reality is that all the resolutions of the European Parliament are conditioned by national considerations, nonetheless powerful because they are undeclared.

Two effects of national interference are constantly seen: one is the dilution of resolutions to take account of particular national concerns; the other is the inclusion in discussions of items which have very little significance outside one or two member states and which are firmly rooted in a singular legal and cultural tradition. In itself this is often no bad thing. It means that the Parliament remains responsive to local demands and concerns and does not develop a policy of its own with no relevance to grassroots society. However, inevitably those nations with the largest groups of MEPs soon come to dominate the thinking and the legislative language of the Parliament. Once again the institution revolves around the preoccupations of the Franco-German alliance which between them accounts for nearly 30% of the members; more varied and diverse than at the Council of Ministers and Commission level because naturally the spread of opinion is greater among the different parties represented. Nonetheless it is hard in such a structure for common platforms within the groups to be agreed without significant national dissent and therefore, inevitably, very difficult for members to reach out to embrace the concerns of countries other than their own, except on specific issues where a committee is dealing with a particular subject in isolation. While proposals are often put forward by a cross-party and trans-national coalition at the committee level, as soon as they come to the floor of Parliament in plenary session the usual rules of the national game apply.

Because Parliament is so nationally sensitive it risks missing out on two areas of allegiance which are of vital importance for the development of a European agenda that reaches beyond the historical views of the member governments. One is the European level itself. The Parliament, by its democratic nature the normal channel between the citizen and the legislative process, risks failing to meet the aspirations of those who work to secure a union sensitive to the cross-border networks of a civil society. There are many people who, while fully valuing their own national traditions and administrative systems, nonetheless want to help Europe fulfil its joint potential. In individual subject areas – whether industrial, cultural or environmental – they are connecting with each other with an imaginative dynamism which few of the institutions have either the vision or the structures to match.

The other level at which the European Parliament is failing to meet the challenges set by European integration is that of the local community, whether it be a national region, a rural area or a city. Individual members of course have home allegiances which gives those places particularly favoured status. There is, however, no formal representation that cements the relationship between an MEP and an individual community. The exception, as so often, is Britain which, by retaining its constituency system and resisting the adoption of proportional representation, falsifies the strength of the vote of the two largest political parties but does ensure a degree of ownership and loyalty between the MEPs and voters. Because the list system is not operated, there is an onus on the member to represent all the people in the home constituency, whatever their political opinion and regardless of whom they voted for. While this creates something analogous to the American local interests problem referred to above, it does provide a degree of democratic legitimacy linking the individual MEP with individual voters. It also provides an opportunity for MEPs to champion issues which might not be of great importance to their national parties but which matter a lot to voters in the constituency. The neatness of this theory is spoilt, though, by the utterly inadequate information that reaches voters about the European Parliament. Few local newspapers or other media carry news or stories about the Parliament and the issues are so far removed from normal discussion that journalists and their audiences have very little understanding of the subjects even when there is coverage. The constituencies, 500,000 voters in each, are too large for the member to make an effective local impact. A depressingly small proportion of the electorate bother to turn out for European voting, and of those that do an even more dismal number are capable of naming their MEP at any stage.

Across the continent the lack of accountability undermines the authority and influence of the one new European institution which the people have a say in constituting. All the other bodies are appointed by governments or staffed by their representatives. It is hardly surprising, therefore, that any allegiance to the concept of European consciousness remains stuck at either the hardest of material or the vaguest of intellectual levels. The Maastricht Treaty recognized that such a deficiency is dangerous and attempted to establish a forum which could give some voice at least to politicians who represented something other than the member states. The Committee of the Regions, however, is another appointed rather than directly elected body and while its allegiances are properly local it has still to define how it should respond to the international agenda other than by pushing the claims of local authorities to the structural funds.

The real deficit, however, is in responding to the strongest and oldest set of allegiances of all; the ones which explain why the Europe envisioned by the citizen for the twenty-first century is very different from that imagined by national governments and parliamentarians and one which fills them with dread when they contemplate it. This is regional Europe, a patchwork of nation-alities and identities which the national states thought they had absorbed and assimilated until they were little more than curiosities for tourists. Even the strong nationalist resurgence that went with the romantic movement from the middle of the eighteenth century onwards did not succeed in threatening the basic structure of the major powers which were consolidating themselves at very much the same time. Just how cultural history can move in opposite directions simultaneously is shown in France, where a new interest in historical identity and folk tradi-tions coincided with the educationally violent imposition of

Francophone standards after the 1789 revolution; ironically a popular revolt which turned out to be even less tolerant of linguistic diversity than even Louis XIV's aristocratic centralized regime had been.

In precisely the same way that national interest is invoked when European union seems to threaten identity, by overlaying decisions which appear to remove national accountability, so the regional nations balk at the assumption that national governments always know best. For many of them the European Union is an opportunity rather than a threat; an opportunity to diminish the relevance of the nation state by federating within the European Union on their own account. These mini-nations are often differentiated by language and sometimes race from the host nation of which they are nominally a part. Often their participation in that nation is a result of conquest rather than integration and the cultural identity which persists defines them as different and marks out a territory with the potential for independence to prove it. This potential was of fantasy status until the advent of European union because they are too small to support their own economic infrastructure on their own.

Union in Europe changes all that. Suddenly the member states of the Union are no longer the inevitable structures within which such smaller sub-nations have to operate. A united Europe offers all the potential for economic and monetary cohesion, redistribution of money, transport infrastructure and educational standards that in the past had to be filtered through a larger nation. In a peaceful democratic Europe defence against neighbours is no longer a threat, so the military inconsequence of tiny countries does not matter. Similarly foreign policy is only relevant to them in terms of relations with each other. Major external relations questions – aid budgets, UN and intercontinental issues – can be left quite equably to the European Union itself. So far this re-grouping has taken place at the level of non-governmental organizations, and semi-official networks of local and regional authorities.

The same motivations which are redefining borders in the old Soviet empire and which tore apart Yugoslavia are at work on a milder scale in western Europe too. They do not, and are not likely to, threaten the position or the existence of the member states in the short term. Over a period of thirty years, though, these shifts may well result in the nation states being modified to a degree where the authority they hold when regional autonomy and European level harmonization are taken into account verges on the ceremonial. Not every region in Europe, if it has a significant degree of autonomy, will see itself as a replacement for the nation state, nor will it trumpet a separate cultural identity. So even if the exact constitutional mechanisms are similar in a decentralized federal Europe, the reality of regional identity will vary enormously from region to region.

Spain and Belgium have already begun to move in this direction. Regions with an historical identity, reinforced by language or dialect, already enjoy a degree of autonomy which is only semantically different from nationhood to save the face of the central Spanish and Belgian governments. The Catalans, Basques, Walloons and Flemish with different degrees of fervour present themselves to the outside world as though the next tier of national government barely exists.

Many others have similar aspirations. In France, Brittany, Alsace and Provence have the potential to be countries with much stronger identity than the current regional formation allows them to articulate. In Britain the cessation of most of Ireland seventy-five years ago started the process of English retreat which Scotland and Wales are increasingly keen to emphasize. Britain's peculiar relationship to international sport, as the country where an extraordinary number of games had their origin, has meant that its internal nations already have an autonomy in the sporting area which they lack almost entirely in the political.

Just how complex this array of alternative allegiances could become can be seen by the strange anachronisms which have been left over by crumbling empires, particularly those of France, Portugal, Britain and Spain. The French constitutional arrangement for its remaining territories means that St Pierre et Miquelon, in the mouth of the St. Lawrence river in Canada, are part of the European Union, as are Guadeloupe and Martinique in the West Indies and Réunion in the Indian Ocean. Portugal maintains the Atlantic island groups of Madeira and the Azores on the same basis, while Spain's footholds on the north African coast, Ceuta and Melilla, are as bizarre. It is as if Nice were suddenly admitted to the Organization of African unity. Britain's immensely complicated traditions, however, mean that none of its remaining colonies or, as it prefers to call them, dependant territories, are allowed the same access to either itself or the union. This means that the Channel Islands and the Isle of Man, surrounded by EU states, are not part of any of the European institutions, though technically subordinate to the British government via the Crown as overlord. They use this to their full advantage, maintaining their independence from all conventions and directives and using their status to run low tax economies which successfully undercut the rigid banking structures of the rest of Europe.

Andorra, San Marino, and the principalities of Monaco and Liechtenstein enjoy similar latitude and their relationship with big neighbours is sufficiently peculiar to mean that they are viewed with indulgence as toy-town states, posing no threat but adding some spice and variety to the boring predictability of the rest of big nation Europe. For countries like Catalunya and Scotland such anachronisms provide a perfect excuse for arguing that the present constitutional arrangements of Europe need not be set permanently and that they should have the chance to pursue an arrangement which gives their sense of cultural distinctiveness full expression.

However this is a difficult scenario for the larger member states to accommodate. While the possibility of European political integration offers the smaller countries an opportunity to develop their identities to an unprecedented extent, it can only do so if many of the privileges and determining powers of the larger countries are delegated to joint European institutions. They will argue that if the process is followed to its logical conclusion the sub-division of Europe could be endless, a recipe for constant local conflict not dissimilar to the feuding between petty statelets in the seventh and eighth centuries. While it might begin with Sardinia and Flanders it could well return Italy to its quilt of city states and Germany to its länder without the need for any federal government. The dreams of Garibaldi and Bismarck would disintegrate. Even England, the most fierce country in defending its sense of national energy, could partition. There is already a demand for a degree of regional devolution to match that planned for Wales and Scotland and the local authorities in the counties and boroughs south of the Scottish border have formed themselves into a Northern Assembly with the specific purpose of co-ordinating grant applications to the European union, now an indispensable source of regional development money. The re-creation of Mercia, Northumbria, Elmet and Wessex need not be that far behind.

If small regional countries do want to see a greater level of autonomy within the European institutional framework – autonomy which meets their emotive cultural aspirations – they will have to find a way of reassuring their current host states that the regionalization of the continent will not lead to total frag-mentation. For nations like Scotland and Catalunya the vision of independence within Europe is the answer to many inconvenient questions. The responsibilities which the strengthened European Union would deal with are those which they do not want and can-not afford to take on themselves in any case – macro-economics, free trade, international crime prevention, foreign affairs and external defence.

For France, Spain, England, Italy and Sweden, however, these are precisely the responsibilities which they hold most dear and which give them a status in world affairs which they will not lightly relinquish. Germany holds a position uncomfortably between these seemingly incompatible extremes. As in the United States, whenever an issue arises between the regional states and the federal government the popular backing is for the regions. There are many areas of national life, culture being one of them, where the central regime has only a marginal influence. Together with this is the attitude imbued in the generation that reached maturity during or soon after the 1939-45 war, that Germany should only involve itself fully in international affairs when it does so in partnership; an attitude which is a right and proper reaction to the disastrous results of pan-German expansionism between Bismarck and Hitler. It is also an attitude which explains why Germans, who are no less nationalist in defence of 'Germanness' than the French or British, do not equate that nationalism with the machismo of government. The belief held firmly in Germany that it always knows best, that its constitution and regulations (from citizen registration to brewing standards) are the only logical ones for the European Union to adopt, is tempered by the understanding that its historical record does not naturally endear the country to the rest of Europe. For this reason the path favoured by the regional nations, of devolving authority up from Member States to the European level and down towards smaller entities, is one that does not cause so much agonising in Germany as one might expect (or that it does in the other 'big' nations).

In terms of political evolution the balance between the European Union, the Member States and the regional nations is the most pressing problem the continent has to face. It is a balance which must achieve a measure of national fulfilment for those that feel, with considerable justification, that they have been discriminated against for centuries, which must give the former imperial powers a strong sense of their own continued importance, and which must allow Europe to develop with enough internal cohesion to give it external influence comparable with America and Asia.

With the exception of Europe's external standing, which is entirely a matter of trade competitiveness and military capability, these conditions are principally about cultural security. If any group, or any individual for that matter, feels that its ability to be in control of its own affairs is in danger, whether these affairs be material or a matter of self-expression, it will not tolerate the interference, even if the threat is imaginary. In the case of Europe the material benefits of integration are acknowledged and even where they are in dispute the arguments for and against are sufficiently balanced for the outcome to be undamaging. Self-determination is the value under threat.

The test is, therefore, whether Europe can provide the reassurance to all its constituent groups that their identity and cultural values will not be devalued where they do not clash with the fundamental rights of others (i.e. the sort of 'cultural right' claimed by Inkatha Zulus and US right-wing militias to carry spears or guns would have to be a right too far). Further, Europe has to recognize, as so many members states are loath to do, that it is made up not just of native citizens of itself but of people who have arrived in Europe from all over the world for a variety of legitimate and honourable reasons. One of these reasons may well be economic opportunity, a reason which is deemed reprehensible by Europe's interior ministers (as Germany's indefensible guest worker regulations attest) but which is surely not. If one of the prime reasons for Europe's single market is to ensure a combination of freedom of movement with fair employment practices and human rights, it is hardly surprising that people from other countries want the same thing. Whatever the reason for immigrant or non-Europeans living here, to fail to win their allegiance will be just as dangerous to the future cohesion of the continent as it would be to alienate a powerful Member State.

There is much more to Europe than ethnic Europeans. Africans began settling after they served in the Roman legions. Moorish colonizers have given southern Spain much of the character which now defines its culture. The labour shortages that followed the successful attempt by Europe to destroy two generations of the native workforce (and many thousands of its colonial subjects) in two world wars meant that rebuilding the continental economy could not have been carried out without inviting millions of people from outside to come and help. After decades of discrimination and abuse they have been given little reward for their achievement, confined in almost every country to the lowest paid jobs and the most miserable of the housing – and this century Europe has pioneered the design of homes without soul or aesthetic excuse. The simultaneous collapse of Empire, with colonial powers too often failing badly in the task of equipping those they conquered with the means or the structures to secure a reasonable standard of living in a just society, has ensured that further millions have taken up their rights to settle in Europe at a time when, with all its disadvantages, it still offers a lure strong enough to be worth the struggle of resettlement. All this was true in the 1960s. Since then however, the children of these settlers (they have being doing nothing else, it must be remembered, than those Europeans who crossed to America in their millions to escape tyranny and poverty; so it is proper to call them settlers rather than to use the more derogatory term 'immigrants') have grown up as Europeans with few reasons to feel wanted in the country of their birth and residence. It would be unfair to say that their allegiances lie elsewhere, because they contribute an immense amount to the society and are as French, British or Italian as any from a more ancient wave of incomers. But it would be true to say that for many the daily antagonism and discrimination they face – whatever the law may provide – means that allegiances to race, original country or religion are often more powerful than those to the country of settlement, let alone the concept of a coherent Europe.

This should not come as much of a surprise. After all, when white colonialists from Europe settled abroad it took generations, often two or three centuries, for them to be convinced that they belonged there – and that was with all the advantages of being dominant and rich compared to the native population. When the degree of degradation suffered by settlers in Europe is taken into account it is remarkable that so many have built such rewarding lives, and that they continue to enrich and enliven cultural and economic activity in ways without which Europe would be an even duller and poorer place. However, it would be naive and dangerous to pretend that alienation and disillusion are not far too strong. There are too many who have been left to feel that they have no stake in European society and no hope of finding anything better anywhere else. Not only is this an absurd waste of creativity and talent, it is a constant reminder of the immaturity of European political rhetoric. If there is a serious intention to make the continent saner and more solid, the allegiances of the disadvantaged settlers in Europe must be harnessed with imagination to opportunity and full social participation. The police, border guards and petty officials that serve states must be made to learn to put aside their suspicion of those who look and sound different from themselves. As anybody who has encountered the French and Spanish police, British and Dutch immigration, or German city bureaucrats will know, there is precious little tolerance of those who are clearly other fellow European citizens, let alone those who might be from somewhere else, especially if it is a place of which a European country used to be overlord.

56

To awaken European consciousness among people who have every reason to develop it is proving hard enough. To engender it in people who have consistently been insulted and let down by Europe might be thought of as nearly impossible. Yet that is what must be done. The alternative is to perpetuate the place of the outsider in and around the major cities and to consign a growing proportion of people, angry and distrustful, to the margins, physical and social. When allied to the potent catalyst of unemployment and domestic insecurity, the mixture will be – already is – explosive. The world of terrorism, religious extremism and National Fronts will seem the only haven for those whose belief in peaceful co-existence has been tested beyond endurance.

Much can be done with better social conditions, improved job prospects, education that leads to decent careers, more understanding among those enforcing regulations and environmentally sensitive building. This will be wasted, though, unless it is bound firmly to a process of making people feel that they belong, wherever they come from, and that their culture is a positive element in European society. It will not be enough to install a Minister for Rock Music or to protect minority languages. On a daily level the potential of ideas and means of expression, of dress, music, language and movement, will have to be explored with open minds and generous hearts. For those who find it quite hard enough to make themselves heard in a difficult climate of fierce international competition it will be a hard test, which Europe must pass. It will not be enough to invent governmental structures for political and monetary cohesion. Unless, to use the word enshrined in the Maastricht Treaty, all the cultures *in* Europe as well as *of* it 'flower', the edifice will always be unstable, a triumphal arch made of icing sugar.

Allegiance is the key. The hope must be that Europeans will be able to find an allegiance to the future that is as strong as the allegiances, so complex, so multi-layered, to the past. Those who understand society best know that allegiances are at their most dangerous when they are concealed, when they are felt but not expressed, or when a particular allegiance is adopted without any historical basis because it allows a fear to be dealt with. Somehow opinion-formers – not just politicians but journalists, artists and teachers – need to help people to discover a set of allegiances which embrace those of the past and bond the multifarious traditions of Europe by consent. Without gaining affectionate, not just pragmatic, allegiance the construction of Europe will be a temporary and unhappy affair.

IV
Abusing Culture

Sweet is the apple smell of other languages
And trusting are the rivers where the trout dance.

Irina Ratushinskaya,
Letter Home

Culture is a source of pride and a cloak for fear. It is the depository
of all the barriers of the past and the garden for future cohesion.
It can generate extraordinary energy but block the simplest of
initiatives. It offers a path to a common European consciousness
that goes deeper than the realization that one is identified as not
from the Far East (though many new Europeans are). The political
aims will not be achieved unless the cultural doubts are assuaged.
This is the message of the previous chapters. How to set about
the assuaging is the task for the rest of this book.

The Treaty of Maastricht recognizes this message by including
in its provisions a duty for the European Union to support the
flowering of culture and to take cultural consequences into
account in all its policy making. The Council of Europe has always
recognized that the care of culture was one of its principal duties.
Both risk failure, however, by stating – and incorporating the
assumptions that lead from the statement in their policies – that
there is something that could be termed a common European
cultural heritage. This commonalty implies that there is and
always has been a sense of a European consciousness and that it
just needs to be awakened for all the people of the continent to
discover their true brotherhood. This is a fallacy. There is no
common culture. Instead there are a multiplicity of responses to
a series of ideas and preoccupations that swept across borders as

59

effectively as the military empires themselves. These ideas were adopted and transformed to fit local cultural and political conditions. Sometimes the results bore striking resemblance to each other. Often the cultural responses were cross-referenced to produce effects which were more than the sum of their local parts. But always these ideas were subjected to a cultural filtering that left them distinctive to the locality.

Where a general picture can be drawn it is clear that the responses to the common ideas current at any particular time follow broadly the generic categories of peoples. So the Renaissance in Italy, where it began as early as the end of the thirteenth century as soon as the Latin world started to reassert itself after a thousand years of Germanic expansion, was very different from its character in Northern Europe. There it led to religious and social conclusions nearly three hundred years later – by which time Italy was into the mannerism of the counter-reformation – which would have amazed those Italian thinkers who had begun to re-evaluate their classical heritage so long before.

The Renaissance was surely not an expression of common European heritage at all. It was, instead, a manifestation of the resurgence of the influence of southern culture as the Gothic, and therefore Germanic, period came under the thrall of Catholicism. The kings of the mediæval north now found themselves subject to a Roman world view which they could no longer systematically control, though they struggled hard to do so. This struggle showed itself in the Great Schism, with the papacy split between factions in Rome and Avignon as France and Germany tried to make the institution their own. However, the battle for domination of the Papacy weakened its hold on the City States of Italy, allowing them to explore their imperial past with a freedom and self-confidence missing for eight hundred years. When the Papacy re-emerged as a significant independent force it was with a more Italian character than had been possible between the sixth and fifteenth centuries, a character shaped by the city-based Renaissance that had grown up around it.

The northern phenomenon of the Reformation was a markedly different reaction to Renaissance ideas. The countries east of the Meuse and around the North Sea had good reasons to want to distinguish their culture from the increasingly Latinate development of expanding France. They reverted to a church system scarcely less corrupt or oppressive than Catholicism, but at least ostentatiously separate and under local control. In this reading the word mediaeval makes sense; for the middle ages to be the middle of something there must be a before and after. They become the period of Germanic dominance between the conquest of the Roman empire and its re-emergence as classicism at the beginning of the seventeenth century.

Since Europe has no common culture, the ideas which swept across it did so not only at different times but in clear contradiction to each other. So the emergence of romanticism happens as classicism reaches its peak; nationalism becomes a potent force just as educated northerners discover the glories of the ancient world on the Grand Tour; the new scientific order of Copernicus and Galileo gains acceptance just as religious intolerance is at its most dogmatic and destructive.

Each culture in Europe only adopts a new set of ideas and influences when it is ready to do so either because it, itself, has reached the end of one developmental phase or because it is in too weak a state to resist pressure from outside. As a result ideas take a long time to spread across the continent, reflecting the social, political and economic conditions of the local cultures they infest. Sometimes a strong culture will adopt and harness a new idea with alacrity quite simply because it is ready and resilient enough to do so: Britain and the industrial revolution is a case in point. Sometimes exhaustion and the threat of national social dis-integration demands a radical rethinking. For Germany this was true after each of the wars it lost after 1870; adopting imperialism, fascism and Europeanism respectively with typical fervour.

Movements take on the characteristics of the cultures through which they advance. So the old Germanic notion of aristocracy, which dominated Europe in its Norman and Frankish form from the ninth century onwards, began to be rejected in the Netherlands in the sixteenth century. The rejection spread to Britain in the 1640s, the new movement reaching its extreme form with the levellers and the execution of King Charles I in 1649. An idea, like a virus, spreads intermittently. So 'levelling' only reached

61

France in 1789, Russia in 1917 and Iran and Nicaragua in 1979. In each case the egalitarianism of the initial movement was replaced by an authoritarian oligarchy within two years.

Inevitably the solemn pace at which ideas take root in each culture means that they are out of sequence with each other but share very similar responses even at several centuries' remove. So Britain and the Netherlands adopted the apparently contradictory philosophies of democracy and constitutional monarchy at the end of the seventeenth century. Italy combined them with nationalism after 1861 to produce its first unified kingdom since the fall of the Western Roman empire, while Spain discovered the doctrine as the solution to the aftermath of fascism in 1976. Simultaneously the influence of classical republicanism, exhumed by the colonial Americans as the only progressive response to oppression imposed by a foreign monarchical democracy, was replacing monarchism, beginning in Europe with France in 1870 but not reaching Greece until 1973.

It is becoming increasingly difficult in this discussion to distinguish between culture and politics. Culture determines the politics. It provides the personality of each group or locality which allows the politics to take place, governs the economics by guiding consumer taste and prepares the conditions for war or peace. At present Europe is trying to find a sense of commonality to reinforce its common purpose. The empirical arguments for cohesion, if not for integration, have been won. There is a consensus in favour of open trade relations, political co-ordination, stable financial instruments, commercial and philanthropic partnerships, supranational institutions, networks of all sorts which identify areas for development, which bring together those interested in particular professions or causes.

Missing, however, is any belief that Europeans are one body of people with impulses common in any deeper sense than those which tie all humans; the urge for peace and prosperity. If there is a further common desire it is for other people to mind their own business and let one run one's own affairs without interference or unnecessary regulation. Since the European Union is a great interferer and regulator, usually using the excuse of creating a fair basis for competition policy, those who are most often asked to change their ways to suit the union will never appreciate the demand. This is where culture is often invoked with most passion, and the reason is easy to see. Fair competition policy automatically means homogenising practices that make one set of people different from another. In order to create absolute or even relative fairness such a policy requires those who differ to align their practice with that of the majority, even if the majority practice is disliked or unacceptable to those on whom it is being foisted. When the practice that needs to be changed is relatively invisible or is of clear social benefit – a rule governing the levels of beach cleanliness for safe bathing, for example – there is rarely an objection. When it covers an aspect of a community's way of life, however, which is in some way a definition of its culture then the European Union loses goodwill whenever it suggests such a measure. Real anger is generated because almost inevitably the standard adopted is the one most commonly in use in the Franco-German alliance or at least among the six original members of the European Community. The invitation to join the Union has a myriad small print conditions, all of them requiring newer recruits to alter aspects of their culture which may seem insignificant in themselves but which add up to a severe erosion of communal identity. Of course the experience works the same way for all so that on the rare occasions when German or French practice is the one being forced to change, it is greeted with just as much nationalistic outrage and fury as it would be in Britain or Spain – the German fight over banana quotas is a case in point.

Rather than reopen past arguments it is worth, by way of example, inventing a subject or two which would create massive cultural indignation if it was applied at the centre of the European Union. One would be if the Commission announced that for the sake of consumers and to provide fair competition between retailers all shops should be open all weekend. For Germany, where Christian Democrat politicians have jealously guarded the traditional day of rest on Sunday and for years have opposed a liberalising of the regulations covering Saturdays, this would be a serious assault. To produce the same outrage in France it might be proposed that no alcohol, including wine, could be served before 11.00 am, a rule that would be suggested by Scandinavian countries as part of their attempts to limit drunkenness. For many Frenchman who are by no means drunkards but like to start the day with a baguette, a cup of coffee and a glass of wine, such a rule would be a cultural catastrophe, however fair to Swedish health. It would be the equivalent of abolishing the Spanish siesta on the grounds that it is only reasonable in a single market to expect all business to be open at the same time. Or announcing that the processes which blacken beer are likely to be confused with charcoal production and so henceforth Guinness and other Irish stouts must be made pale.

The officials at the Commission, despite suggestions to the contrary, have more sense than to propose any such thing. To rile Germany, France or Spain so openly, to place their politicians in a position which they would be utterly unable to defend, would be to risk ridicule and rupture on an unacceptable scale. There is not the same squeamishness evident, however, when it comes to altering the cultural practices of countries newer to the Union, less central to its ambitions or less enthusiastic about accelerated integration. It is the suspicion that Brussels always tends to regard the only fair way as the German or French way which causes a lingering feeling of resentment in those parts of Europe geographically or emotionally distant from the Rhine.

Officials are human too. At least some give the appearance of being so. The suggestions they make are often governed by their own cultural experience. In Brussels this may mean that they adhere too closely to the cultural practices of their own home country. It may also mean, though, that if they are part of the new breed of Eurocrat, bred and educated outside the parameters of any one culture, they may try to build a Europe that pays little regard to the niceties of regional diversity, preferring instead to fashion a set of rules which impose more homogenous standards. Both are ultimately destructive approaches. Local traditions will not allow themselves to be tampered with either to standardize or to bring them into line with a model considered superior.

This chapter has been a litany of complaint; complaint that the builders of a coherent Europe prefer to act in the interests of a few member states only; complaint that it is usually seen as easier to force order than to accommodate human diversity; complaint that a technocratic vision of Europe is dictating the way coherence is implemented; finally complaint that a central group of nations believe their political goals must be universal because these nations are so determined to achieve them. However to complain is not the purpose of this text. Although complaining might induce some extra sensitivity it would only be temporary. The Commission, the Bundesbank, together with the French, German and Dutch governments would soon regain the initiative in the conviction that anyone who did not agree was at best whinging, at worst had no interest in a better Europe. A blueprint must be drawn which offers a fresh way of bringing people, not just governments and their regulations, together; one that enhances the cultures of Europe and revels in their peculiarities; one that realizes that it is the very lack of a uniform European culture which gives the continent its inventiveness and dynamism.

To harness that inventiveness constructively, it is important to understand the varying levels of meaning that are attached to the word culture. In a debate where irrational but deeply held positions are at stake it is all too easy to find the participants invoking culture, while meaning significantly different things. At its most politically sensitive culture includes all aspects that are the expression of our defined life style, from whether we live in blocks of flats or half-timbered houses to what we eat for the evening meal and at what time we eat it. It governs our expectations of institutions and officials, what we expect our children to be taught at school and whether we regard living in the countryside as an idyll of contentment that stimulates creativity or as a place so out of touch with the modern world that it is only fit for peasants with no intellectual ambition.

At the industrial level culture includes the myriad ways in which we give ourselves identity and entertainment: how we dress for any occasion, what we listen to, watch and read, how the consumer goods we favour are advertised to us, how news is reported, the typefaces of printed material and public signs with which we feel comfortable. If this book appeared in a typeface that was thought of as overtly American or with a cover that identified it with India, its chances of being taken seriously in Europe would diminish before a word was read.

Making It Home

For the artist and conservator culture is used in both a specific and an unspecific way. It encompasses the heritage of our legacy of buildings, the processes and results of artistic creation and the infrastructure provided for exhibition and performance. When those that regard themselves as the cultural sector are out hunting for finance they are looking for money to help them distribute ideas, not for the advertising of goods and services.

Each cultural level carries with it a different political appeal and, inevitably because it is a matter of self perception, of defiant protectiveness. Unfortunately for those working in the arts and the conservation of the built heritage it is not their level which arouses the political passion which would guarantee them the money they need. The life style level is one for which people will fight and which politicians fail to defend at their peril. Fear that a community's way of life will be changed against its will is subordinate only to threats of deprivation of food and shelter as a justification for war. Indeed people will tolerate great material hardship to protect their culture when it means their way of life.

The industrial level is an increasingly important component of economic success. This, sadly, is not because cultural industries are intrinsically any more loved or interesting than they have ever been – or at least have been since the invention of the cinema and gramophone. Rather it reflects the collapse of manufacturing industry in Europe since the 1930s, a collapse which was caused by the demands of workers for decent conditions, the failure of the banking system to invest generously at home, and by the simultaneous emancipation of previously captive colonial markets. The efforts of Europe to stimulate its own home market have not saved the major part of its manufacturing base but they have been able to encourage employment in small specialist industries and in those which recycle activity, helping society service itself with finances already in the system.

The cultural industries are among the most effective agents of growth in an economy unable to rely on manufacture. They use technology at its most advanced. They are as sustainable at the individual level (writers, potters, designers) as they are at the local (radio stations) or the national (television, film and publishing). Perhaps strangely the cultural industries in general have been slow to move outside their traditional national constituencies. This has been partly because of language barriers, partly too because of national restrictions on the development of broadcasting. However only the music industry has made a continental impact commensurate with its national importance, and then only through the Polygram, Bertelsman and EMI corporations. Those broadcasters which have treated Europe as a potential single market have not been European, but rather American or Australian. The same has been true of publishers and film distributors.

Among the hardware manufacturers Philips stands almost alone as a European rival in its own market to the Japanese and absolutely no European company has made even a dent in the computer industry comparable with the transatlantic IBM, Apple or Microsoft. Fashion companies have taken advantage of the opportunities but to no greater extent than they have of other international markets. Gucci, Dior, Chanel and Laura Ashley have as much to do with Los Angeles, Tokyo and Sydney as they do with Milan, Paris and London. As a result the pride felt in the cultural industries is primarily nationalistic rather than European. Politically they have few friends in the supra-national institutions and an influence on legislation and debate which is pathetically slight considering their economic and social importance.

The built heritage is by its nature a matter for local and national concern and, as has been said above, reflects more the way regional cultures have responded to general common ideas rather than the way European culture has influenced local ideas. Nonetheless it is of continental importance that Venice, the Alhambra, Stonehenge and the boulevards of Paris are given the respect they deserve. These are merely the champion attractions of course, but if Europe is serious about building a consciousness that crosses borders then it must admit that it is just as vital to respect less grandiose sites, whether they be archaeological, grandiloquent or vernacular. In an age of tourism, if not yet of identification with other nations, it is a matter for European concern that the distinct character and significance of the built heritage is given the conservation that will continue to underlie local cultural variation.

Paradoxically it is the artists and their organizations who have shown the greatest awareness that there is potential for truly European cultural activity. It can be argued that this was always the case and that artists and their ideas were always more mobile than their patrons or indeed the taste of the public. Following the few jobs available was one cause of this. However artists of all disciplines have always argued that while national and local roots underpin their work there are no borders of any relevance; indeed that the opposite is true. An artist is judged on inter-nationality of reputation rather than popularity at home, some-thing that applies in very few other professions.

Music, dance and the visual arts have always traversed frontiers without any regard to them. This does not mean that there is no national or regional accent in the work, merely that the vocabulary of the art form is such that the barriers thrown up by spoken language do not apply. Even where they do in theory – in opera or song, for example – the other elements of the work are strong enough to carry the message across borders. Language-based art forms – theatre, poetry and prose – have naturally found it harder to travel. Even now, with a vibrant television market and publishers keen to translate a reasonable number of books, it is common for a writer or actor to be a national icon in one country or linguistic group of countries but utterly unknown in others. Many great French writers do not ripple the surface of the English best-seller lists and the same is true of Germans in Spain or Italians in Sweden. Poets are particularly badly affected by this since it is hard enough to break into the market in the mother tongue, virtually impossible to sell in commercial quantities in another without subsidy.

As theatre has moved in the last fifty years to a style which has more emphasis on movement, gesture and atmosphere and less on the direct meaning of words, so it has become more trans-portable in Europe, especially in venues catering for small intellectual audiences. For mass audiences the packaged musical, interchangeable in detail wherever it is produced, has proved that theatre can jump linguistic barriers, however banal (or perhaps because it appeals to the lowest common denominator) the material. So it is hardly surprising that it has been theatre professionals who have been among the first to build networks across the continent.

Other professions have followed. It has seemed to be a slow process but it was given great impetus by the implementation of the Maastricht Treaty with its inclusion of culture as a legitimate area of interest for the Union for the first time. Once it became clear that the European Parliament and Commission were developing policies that had a direct bearing on the financing and working practices of the arts, many organizations that already existed rejuvenated themselves and others were formed. Now there are European Associations for festivals, symphony orchestras, jazz promoters, textile artists, amateur archaeologists, arts centres in historic venues, arts centres in converted factories, composers, copyright collection agencies, concert artists' agencies, conservatoires, entertainment trade unions and film directors, to name just a few.

The reasons for joining together are many. There is the need to compare practice and experience at a time when the trusted solutions no longer seem to be adequate. Some feel the need to lobby to ensure that EU legislation does not harm their profession or, more positively, to persuade legislators to remove barriers to their wish to work together. Some look for opportunities to extricate funds from the increasingly rich EU programmes. Often these programmes are not specifically aimed at cultural organi-zations but, with some deft semantics in interpreting the criteria, they can be adapted to the cultural cause.

This plethora of associations is putting European cohesion into practice without the political burden carried by the state apparatus. Because the common interest is limited to professional activity that can be shared, there is not the same fear of being taken over that permeates political life. Instead a raft of new partnerships is being built, new projects are being launched and skills exchanged which will take arts practitioners into exciting new territory based on multilateral relationships that are far more complex than the old mechanisms of bilateral cultural exchange.

The advantage such professional networks have over the European Union institutions is that by their nature they cannot go further than offering opportunities. The lives of their members remain as individual and locally-based as they wish. The Council of Europe has had a policy of encouraging such networks for over a decade. It too recognizes that the old formulae of cultural exchange, designed as an adjunct to the ambassadorial system and nurtured in the cold war, is no longer adequate for an interdependent Europe. Because the Council of Europe is not based on the politics of economics but is instead a guardian of the values of civilization, it has been able to see much faster than the European Commission that the cultural sector has a crucial role to play in the creation of a concept of Europe that is coherent, but that does not threaten to usurp the psychological territory of nationhood by superimposing Franco-German political control. Its much wider membership of forty-two countries, compared to the fifteen of the EU, makes the management of such control an absurdity.

The Council of Europe may turn out to have been one of the great missed opportunities of politics. For years it was the agent for the western powers' agreements on human rights and democracy; maintained as a monument to be exhibited to the authoritarian regimes of the Soviet bloc. As the European Union developed and gathered to it the dynamics of political integration so the interest, and with it the will to put money into the Council of Europe, began to dwindle. France and Germany saw it as an institution which could involve countries superfluous to the EU without watering down their version of an integrated 'inner Europe'. Britain sees the Council as a bit of a waste of time just as it too often similarly regards bodies which concentrate on intelligent discussion rather than the arrangements for making money.

Other countries inside the EU consider the Council a benevolent missionary for good intentions. Only those not distracted by the European Union's more pressing agenda, which tends to mean those that feel a bit left out of the political scene in Brussels, give the Council serious attention. For those who have not yet joined the Union – like Cyprus, Hungary, Malta and Iceland – or those who are just finding their feet as independent countries, like the new Slav states of central and eastern Europe, the Council is much more significant. It provides a source of expertise, of recognition of regional status and nationhood, a certificate of their wish to be seen as countries with liberal credentials (though the record on human rights of several of them is less than pristine) and a forum to engage with the richer EU powers with a measure of equality.

The Council of Europe, however, remains the poor relation of the European Union, not just in financial terms but also in terms of the attention it receives from Ministers and officials. There is a blindness to the potential of the organization which shows that its members are too preoccupied with the challenges and threats of Union affairs to have time for the subtler discussions of Strasbourg. Because the Council of Europe reviews human rights, democracy, culture and education and brings together in its Parliamentary Assembly the sitting elected members of national parliaments, it is concerned with the way in which we behave towards each other to a far greater extent than the EU, which is more interested in how we trade and who has the power of legislative control. The EU is an instrument of power, the Council of Europe is an instrument of co-operation.

If the real goal of European society is to have a continent where there is no need for territorial defensiveness, where there is mutual prosperity without dour uniformity, where each layer of loyalty is not challenged by the demands of the economically and demographically powerful, it is to democracy and cultural values that we must look with urgency. For this a better resourced Council of Europe will be a preferable instrument to the self-interested artillery of the European Union, an invention that if it cannot satisfy the political imperatives of German and French regimes will soon outlive its usefulness. So far in all the moves to bind Europe together culture has been misunderstood, mis-handled and misrepresented.

The Union States have failed to invent a European culture to replace the nations', whether the nations are independent or subsidiary. They have tried to harness the superficial trappings of culture to their propaganda aims, either for or against the concepts of closer union. They have invoked culture as the means by which the people of Europe will come to love the Union without understanding that it is precisely a love of their real local and

71

personal culture which makes people wary of such a blatant piece of manipulation. They, the member states, fail to realize the complexities of the cultures they are trying to replace. A festival or two, a few multi-national training orchestras, a gala performance carrying the name of the union, pointless pieces of facile entertainment like *Jeux sans Frontières* or the Eurovision Song Contest do little to make people feel more European. Instead they provide arenas for people to feel nationalistic together, to affirm their differences without having to be aggressive. So far Europe has abused culture and is now liable to pay the price. Sullen citizens, who are tired of being promised material gain that is never quite delivered, are losing faith in the projects that so inspire the political establishment.

The leaders of Italy, France, Spain, Germany and the Netherlands are increasingly baffled to find that while everybody wants a free and open Europe, they are less enchanted than they should be with the model being forced upon them. Without a serious attempt to rethink the basis of Union, the price exacted by citizens once the formidable bulk of Chancellor Kohl has left the scene is likely to be too much for the structures of the union to withstand. While there cannot be a union without political will, economic convergence and institutions with decision-making powers, equally a union which fails to win over hearts as well as wallets will not survive.

V

Using Culture

'Tis hard, my Friend, to write in such an Age,
As damns not only Poets, but the Stage.

John Dryden,
To My Friend, The Author

It was when the playwright Vaclav Havel appeared unhindered at the head of demonstrations in Prague that for many the collapse of Cold War politics seemed complete. Only a few months before, despite all the Reagan-Gorbachev summitry, the Czech regime had been confident enough of its security to imprison him. In so many of the countries of the Soviet empire the artists were, in theory, soft individual targets without military or political power, easy for the governments to crush. In reality they were the most durable harbingers of change. The release of the young Ukrainian poet Irina Ratushinskaya in 1986 had signalled that for all the talk of Star Wars, Gorbachev's agenda might be different from that of Brezhnev, Andropov and Chernenko. When the conductor of the Leipzig Gewandhaus Orchestra, Kurt Masur, stepped in to urge a non-violent end to East Germany only days after it celebrated its fortieth anniversary it was the first moment when it seemed certain that it could not survive. In Romania the constant drip of criticism by the country's greatest actor, Ion Caramitru, was the most effective reminder that, under Ilescu, there was a long way to go before the Ceaucescu structures were irrevocably demolished. Just as the civil war in Bosnia-Herzogovina reached its bloodiest period, I remember sitting alone in the ruins of the amphitheatre of the shrine of Delphi as Caramitru stood at its centre and ranged through Shakespeare's plays for speeches

73

which expressed the horror of the events, but also the determination to achieve real freedom. Throughout the decade since the Reagan-Gorbachev summits signalled the potential for change, it was the artists who embodied the spirit of peaceful progress and fulfilment.

In each of these nations, though, the process of rediscovery and free thinking involved a sense of delight at the removal of an imposed international system and the rebirth of an essentially nineteenth-century concept of nationalism. However, all the efforts at international co-operation since 1945 – the creation of institutions and civil rather than military alliances – have been aimed at overriding the divisiveness of nationalism in a period which has seen the creation of more sovereign nations than ever before. At the level of governments and officials these efforts have been a remarkable success. In political terms too those who have striven to bring the peoples of Europe together have been rewarded as two generations in Western Europe have grown up in peace, as the undemocratic regimes of Greece, Portugal, Spain and the eastern bloc have given way to more legitimate forms of government, and as the intellectual debate has found a consensus that there can no longer be a justification for national interest to end in war.

And yet, despite the nobility of the aims and the determination of those who have built these extraordinary structures, unparalleled in world history, the fact that the unity has been imposed on society by its leaders, instead of emerging in a slower but more organic process, has meant that the emotional or human belief in a European consciousness has been inadequate. It is plausible to argue that this is just a matter of time; that as people get used to new arrangements they will, just like bank notes which caused such a furore when they superseded coins in the nineteenth century, be seen as normal, even natural. That is what politicians must hope. However there is no guarantee because, as I have argued, the instincts behind public affairs reach back a great deal further and deeper than the history books dare to suggest.

Such a failure is not a failure of leadership but of comprehension. For a professional it is always difficult to realize just how ignorant of one's profession those who do not share it really are.

So for professional Europeanists the notion that their enthusiasm for and mastery of the intricacies of multilateral policy making is not only incomprehensible but often regarded as positively dangerous by a large number of citizens who have decent but different concerns can be baffling. The result is one that wounds the integrators deeply. The more energetically they push for a common purpose and the mechanisms to implement it, the more defensive the citizens become and the more they reach for the security of their old nationalism. In turn, as large elements within nation states find ways to demonstrate their separate identity, so the nation states themselves become prone to subdivision and Balkanization, as people who held an historical grievance against them use the same arguments and emotions to galvanize their own cause. Even if new institutions, or stronger versions of already existing ones, are successfully launched, the danger of fracture will remain. If the strains of integration are too great because of economic downturn or political misunderstanding Europe will quickly revert to its usual tribal self.

To prevent such a miserable outcome political leaders must learn to restrain their natural instincts, which are themselves schizophrenic. It may prove an impossibly acrobatic task to satisfy the demands of national identity and international statesmanship at the same time. Instead they will have to put less effort into the mechanics of legislative union and more into the processes which can enable citizens to develop their own ideas and identities; harnessing individual aspirations rather than assuming that a group mentality can be imposed from above for more than a short period of five to ten years.

These processes are and must be seen as cultural. Any attempt to dilute cultural identity and try adapt to the American and Australian 'melting pot' approach will not work in Europe because of the strong affinity between territory and language. The industrial model which tries to make uniform products available everywhere will undermine these territorial boundaries but it will also induce a sense of being taken over; of having nothing to offer that is special. When one goes to Scotland one wants to find a whisky that is not available in every supermarket. When one goes to the south of France there is no pleasure in finding that the pottery is no different from anything that can be found for half the price at home. If the cultural industries continue to follow the export market model they will eventually succeed only in suppressing tourism and the spending associated with it, as travellers only travel for the weather and come home empty-handed and disappointed by the sameness of it all. An homogenized political nation called Europe would be just as unsatisfactory.

On the other hand if cultural difference is celebrated in as many different ways as possible, there may be results which confound the doctrines of Eurocrats but which every national and regional politician knows as a matter of true instinct; advantageous results which countries such as Ireland have already exploited to their intense economic and social benefit. If the emphasis on culture is celebratory and non-aggressive (in other words if it is seen as a matter of pride but not victory) then other nationalities will join in the celebrations.

An example of how this should *not* be done is seen each time the European soccer championships are held. To beat Germany becomes the aim, not just of teams but of nations. As it becomes clear that Germany's combination of talent, aptitude and organization will be triumphant once again Europe does unite after a fashion, but only in terms of being virulently anti-German. The sport becomes a metaphor for German economic and political dominance and the metaphor is resented no less than the reality. The German people see and are hurt by this show of general antagonism and they react in their daily lives, business and politics by being even more determined to place themselves in an unassailable position and to retreat into a cocoon of Germanness which is impregnable.

Ireland provides the alternative example. It is perhaps inevitably easier for the Irish because they have not been in a position to inflict invasive violence against anybody else since the fifth century (leaving aside the intractable problem of the IRA and the British). Ireland has been intent for much of the last century on establishing its identity through the celebration of its culture. It has made late but intensive efforts to secure its language (with, it must be said, only limited success; Gaelic is still not used as a working language as much as it was before the great famine of the 1840s). It has used tax incentives to encourage writers, film makers, craftsmen and musicians to exploit its traditions and landscape. While it has failed to support theatre and dance to the same degree, it has used the diaspora of Irish descendants around the world to make sure that Irish pubs, Irish music and Irish writing is continuously fashionable. The Irish have used the combination of Celtic nostalgia and grievance against their neighbour's empire to great effect, such that the grievance is now irrelevant and they can be secure in their cultural popularity. So successful has the policy been that in Hollywood films, great barometers of how cultures are seen in the popular consciousness, you will almost never find a bad Irishman and you will equally almost never be offered a British or German hero. For the majority of Americans, despite the German and British ancestry of so many of them, the only regularly acceptable presentation of characters from their old countries is as villains. An American has to have the main part, of course, but it is always allowable to have a lovably Irish support.

Ireland is a small nation and it is the small nations which will have to be promoted if the sense of cultural security is to be installed. If for a change the larger nations can be made to realize that they themselves are a coalition of cultural identities while the smaller nations are more, but never totally, homogenous, then a feeling of rough cultural equality can be nurtured. The cultural identities need not, indeed should not, be equated with ethnic purity. A sense of belonging, of being at home, is what is needed and that can come from residence, upbringing, settlement and preference as much as ancestry. Individuals are capable of having three or more cultural identities simultaneously. Societies need to learn the same multiplicity and then to build it into the image they present of and to themselves.

Celebrating the historical, ethnic, linguistic and aspirational diversity of Europe is often talked about as an essential pre-requisite of a stable future. Unfortunately there is a tendency on the part of governments to assume what might be called the Dutch position; one in which they are automatically the logical unit of comparison – that theirs is the most misunderstood, undervalued, endangered and vulnerable culture, threatened by domination from above and regional faction from below. In fact almost all cultures feel like this. It is why one of the few areas of undisputed agreement among the Member States of the European Union is that they must retain the right to manage their own cultural affairs. They understand them so badly, however, and so manage them so badly, that it is the nation states themselves which are placing their cultures in jeopardy. The danger comes from two simple misconceptions; that you can defend national identity without paying nationally for its cultural manifestations, and that the visible exhibition of the culture – whether it be in performance, the broadcast or printed media, a gallery, museum or preserved in the landscape – is little more than entertainment and so worthy of minimal political and financial status. Yet the same national politicians who bemoan the loss of their national identity will spend enormous sums of money devising and sustaining an armoury to defend the smallest measure of land defined by an imaginary line.

The arts can be every bit as effective, more effective in the long term, as armies at defending an identity, especially those that have an important role in establishing cultural awareness – poetry and novels, film, television and radio drama, architecture and music (I would argue that sculpture and contemporary painting are less identified with any particular culture and that theatre has an internal examining role within a culture rather a defining one). It is worth suggesting that one of the strongest reasons for Germany's fast post-war rehabilitation and its ability to reinvigorate its political and economic structures was its determination that a strong cultural infrastructure was essential. Despite the realization that they had been beaten and had perpetrated appalling damage on their own and other lands following a criminal dream, Germans were able to fall back on a cultural identity invested in a body of artistic work which was clearly valuable and worthy of their confidence. If Beethoven and Goethe were still unassailable then Stockhausen and Herman Hess could emerge from the rubble. The health of late twentieth-century Germany was as much due to its ability to draw on the security of its cultural life – an assurance that normality was possible and that German ideas still had a role – as to its industrial performance.

Very much the same can be said of several other societies emerging from the trauma of defeat or revolution. Russia, the Czech Republic, Bosnia and Estonia have found in recent years that the quality of their cultural life offers a source of pride and energy that can hold a society together when everything else has been falling apart. For the Czechs it was the music and the message of Dvorak, the plays of Havel, the novels of Kundera and the films of Forman that held the spirit together. In Sarajevo, a place where all the fault lines of Europe converge to produce forces of volcanic destructiveness, many have said that it was their ability to share music and poetry which gave them the hope that a fresh start was possible.

Most of Europe is now in a less extreme situation but that does not mean that its economic and political goals are any easier or less traumatic to achieve. Each country needs a different formula for cultural security because each has a different series of fissures in its social and historical structure. France needs to rediscover the non-francophone potential of its regions and minorities. Spain as a whole needs to follow the lead given by Barcelona in discovering the confidence which the array of magnificent old cultures can give. Britain needs to revive the richness of the English regions to rescue them from the surly identity they now have, defined by hatred of London and the South East (themselves in fact two regions just as much in need of a revived and cohesive identity) and to allow Scotland, Wales and Cornwall the respect and self-determination they crave.

Italy is perhaps the one country where the problems are more to do with the culture of administration rather than the administration of culture but still it too needs to find ways of conserving its riches while allowing room for innovation. A more outward looking mentality would help. It is often noticeable that Italians behave entirely differently when they cross the Alps, as though they have left behind a burden of stress which allows them to think calmly and clearly. Oddly for northern Europeans the reverse is true. The light and warmth of Italy is an instant tonic to the mind.

Poland and the other Baltic countries, along with Slovakia and Romania, must learn to recognize the strength that the variety of peoples in their country will give their cultures in the future and must stop trying to manufacture an identity by discriminating against those who do not fit narrow definitions, usually because they are said to be ethnically different. This is an attitude no different in its reasoning from Nazism. Picking which of your citizens are eligible to take part in a democracy is a process fraught with jeopardy. To base such a process on a defence of culture is to infect the culture as surely as a cancer cell induces those around it to mutate. It is to forfeit all the benefits of culture and turn the society back to the false history that leads to misery and conflict.

Cultural confidence and security is not a recipe for turning Europe into a tourist theme park for each other or for American and Japanese travellers, assumptions and cameras at the ready, to invade like a flock of non-indigenous vampires. We all know that while tourism is a welcome addition to the economy it can disrupt the natural life of a community, destroy the very characteristics that the tourists have come to enjoy in the first place and leave the society feeling that it is parasitic, only to be defined by its ability to act as temporary servants to those who regard the locals as a variant of a zoo. There is a fine line between making the most of cultural assets so that the potential rewards are reaped and debasing them so that by their very promotion confidence and security are undermined and their value to the culture is lost. Small coastal communities are most at risk and most of those in southern France, Spain, Portugal and Greece are already lost. Only a cataclysmic recession, a vicious demolition gang and a mass exodus can return them to a better state and it is probably too high a price too pay. Even that might not work. Innocence is hard to regain. Other communities are in danger too. Cultural tourism is suburbanising Stratford-upon-Avon and swamping Prague. The one thing Mozart was spared when he lived in Salzburg, much as he hated the place, was the glutinous excess of the Mozart memorial industry. Sometimes the legacy of a great artist would be much better if it was confined to his or her art. Europe must not become a chain of visitor centres and souvenir shops. Of course it must share its cultures and inform those who travel to enjoy it. But cultural security is about giving people enough faith in their own intrinsic capability to allow them to be positive participants in shared cultures in the future. It should not degenerate into subservient nostalgia.

If this sharing is to be achieved a great deal of detailed work lies ahead. The nations, encouraged morally and if necessary financially by the European institutions (preferably the Council of Europe after having been voted an increase in funding for its cultural division), should conduct a cultural audit of themselves and their constituent regions. No state would be allowed to pretend (as Britain has on occasion) that it does not have regions because there is no administrative entity, or like France that the hegemony of the French language makes such distinctions irrelevant. The result will be a complicated map, even with several layers of culture covering the same territory, but it will be the first that shows Europe as it is rather than how its rulers have agreed it should be.

As part of the audit there would be a security assessment, looking at the level of confidence or disaffection in each cultural segment and recommending how it should be tackled: with money for cultural activity, administrative recognition, legislative action or simply by way of enabling people to feel that their future is under their own control.

Whatever the action required (and if the job is done properly there will be plenty), agreement will need to be reached about how to implement it. Nations vary in their willingness to make good their intentions. For once ringing phrases and handsome resolutions will not be enough. Cash will have to change hands and laws will have to be enforced. Paradoxically, to heal the divisions between cultures there will need to be a division of resources determined at the European level, which each of those cultures it is designed to help concur with, as incorporating fair and reasonable recognition. Each area will be given a plan to enhance its cultural security and, because such security rests with individuals and their personal psychology, not with administrative authorities, the plan will need to be communicated personally. To be trusted this work had better be left to non-governmental organizations rather than officials or politicians whose stock with the public is at its lowest for many decades.

Subsidiarity is of course the jargon term included in the Treaty of Maastricht to allow for decisions to be made at the appropriate level. However when it comes to cultural programmes the packaged disorder that is European cultural policy has failed to include an understanding of what it means. A jumble of minor funding programmes, the inclusion of building projects some of which are quite cultural in the structural funds, a bundle of youth orchestras and the emblematic endorsement of a couple of cities per year does not amount to a serious attempt to get to grips with the cultural problems of Europe. Nor does it give any real encouragement to Member States and their subsidiary nations to tackle the matter themselves.

A real cultural policy for Europe would seek to ensure that the continent's constituent cultures had the support to survive vigorously. This means badgering the nations to resource them properly and to persuade the Member States that diversity in a society is as beneficial as it is in biology. It does not have to be a threat to the stability of the nation state if it is handled with sensitivity. Up until the present, however, very few of the imperial states of Europe have demonstrated that they can accommodate such a concept.

Once the cultures are secure and vibrant they must be the engines of European cohesion, driving a convoy of projects that, by bringing like-minded cultures together, will inevitably forge new alliances across the continent, sometimes within a Member States, sometimes at considerable distance. There are ways that the European institutions can help them do this that go beyond money and programmes with acronymic labels.

One way would be to monitor the cultural sensitivity of the institutions' own proposals and programmes. Almost inevitably at present documents emanating from the Commission and Council Secretariats reflect the cast of thought of the nationality of the person first writing them. Predominantly the prevailing cultural framework is French or German. Often, subsequent opposition is triggered not so much by the wisdom or lack of it of the proposals themselves as by an automatic cultural response to the manner in which they are expressed. Thus the rhetorical nature of French or the emphasis on rules and restrictiveness in

German administrative parlance, each taken over in some degree by the Benelux cultures, can alienate Nordic, British, Slav or Mediterranean readers from the start. Similarly the clarity and sequential nature of English or Scandinavian proposals can seem to the Francophone mind to be mechanistic or lacking in elegance and finesse. Northern systems, accustomed to framing statutes which must be followed to the letter, find Southern documents absurd, comprised as they often are of high-minded aims and objectives to be achieved by impossible or impractical means. Northerners do not understand that the southern cultures leave the details of implementation far more to the discretion of the relevant authorities, whatever the paper might actually say.

To combat these irritants the institutions need to monitor and adjust proposals before they are presented to Parliaments or Councils of Ministers, vetting them for connotations of cultural snobbery or elements guaranteed to be greeted with a negative reaction. The same is true of correspondence to the institutions from citizens and non-governmental bodies. There must be a new understanding among officials about the significance of methods of expression. Too often sensible and profound proposals from outside Brussels are lost in official inertia because they do not arrive framed to suit the Francophone taste.

The expectations of officials and politicians is one side of the coin. But they in turn have a right to expect a measure of goodwill and co-operation from citizens once their cultural security is assured. From the citizen of a stable Europe this requires a mobility of thought to travel alongside the right to mobility of residence. This is not just a matter of tolerance, though that is important. It is relatively easy to tolerate people even if you heartily dislike them as long as they do not interfere with daily life. Mobility of thought demands rather more; the mental flexibility to retain one's cultural security while feeling comfortable with the way others manage their lives in a different cultural setting. It is remarkably hard to do and even with the best will in the world most of us are very bad at it. Dealing with strange working practices and living restrictions, house renting and banking habits and shopping hours can induce an unreasonably strong resentment. It is all part of feeling lost in a strange land

and the natives are rarely sympathetic. Even with the freedom to work and travel, guaranteed to citizens by the various treaties, there are still procedures of registration and social management which are specifically designed to make the outsider realize that this is not home.

Many of the bureaucratic requirements for moving around between European countries are absurdly circular. For example, civic registration is not available without a residential address, a residential address is not available without a bank account, a bank account is not available without a social security number, a social security number is not available without civic registration – and all in an unknown or unfamiliar language. Only the most confident or desperate will exercize their rights to travel and work in such a deliberately antagonistic official atmosphere. Preparing people to avoid culture shock should be one of the main duties of the employment Directorate General of the European Commission. In every territory of the Union it should have an office to offer help and advice to the incoming citizen; helping with the formalities of movement, smoothing the process of getting started in the new society. The locals will not, of course, understand why it is necessary. To them all the peculiar customs are the stuff of normal life, based on assumptions they have shared since childhood. To another EU citizen, however, the schisms of territory and language have meant that moving a few kilometres can be as culturally traumatic as moving to Japan. The result can be disillusionment and hatred where previously there was optimism and trust.

Cultural assumptions and the politics which stem from them reach much deeper and take far longer to form than the speed of communication or the few years between conflicts. It would be nice to think that our mental evolution was faster than our physical but there is no reason to suppose that this is so. We are not as adaptable as viruses or bacteria, able to mutate dramatically within a generation or two. Our dress and technological equipment may change but less superficial indicators do not alter so readily. Cultural identification is, in anthropological terms, the fundamental description of our process of selection and familiar protection. It is a biological necessity, not an intellectual curiosity.

To remove the natural suspicion, to shift into psychological patterns which the mind knows our civilization requires but which our nature tells us is dangerous and incautious, will take more than an advertising campaign or two and some pretty festivals, although these can be useful indicators of intent.

Instead a new approach to education will have to be instilled. It will not produce instant results. Indeed it is likely to take at least four or five generations before the ideas that it carries are accepted readily enough to make an apparent difference in everyday life. That is how long social attitudes take to adapt, however, and there is no point in being impatient. The story of the women's movement, even though accelerated by the dislocations of two world wars and the improvements of contraception, gives a clue. Despite its apparent success the process is far from complete. While women are now legally equal they can be said to be only really equal in misfortune. The movement has introduced a measure of insecurity in men and stress in women which will have to be dealt with in the next two generations, making the passage from one sort of social stability to another a journey of a least one hundred and fifty years.

There is no reason not to start, however. The arts have already done so. Music, dance and the visual arts are taught with reference but not deference to national and cultural boundaries. Indeed they feed off the dynamism which results from cross-fertilization. Cultural purity in the arts soon leads to stagnation and pastiche. Literature, history and theatre, the arts most closely related to emotional identity, have only recently begun to move across territory. Of course there have always been writers with international reputation and universal adoption. This says more about the particular genius of Shakespeare, Molière, Ibsen and Beaumarchais, however, than it does about the way their art forms are taught.

A thorough revision of curricula across Europe is needed if the ignorance of each other's history and culture is to be ameliorated over time. This will be hard to do and it may mean that the sheer volume of knowledge and experience young people will have to ingest will require them to spend a year longer in full time education than they generally do at present. This would be no disaster, though. Already the employment market is asking for ever more highly trained school graduates. The level of scientific and technological sophistication they will need in the next fifty years for a successful career in a computer-driven Europe means that they will anyway have to surrender a year or two. If medical progress continues to deliver longer active life there is no reason why they could not retire a little later to even the equation.

Ever since universal education was introduced there has been an imperial or, later, an anti-imperial slant to the way history, literature and theatre have been taught. In the period of European empires it was the growth of the individual nations which led to the empires that was the basis of teaching. The classical world was covered reasonably thoroughly but in most systems there was a gap, the absurdly labelled dark ages, until the emergence of nations that were recognisable to their imperial citizens. So in Germany detailed teaching began with Charlemagne and the installation of the Holy Roman Empire up until 1914 when history became too uncomfortable. In France it began with Clovis and the emergence of the first Frankish leaders to use the term, in England with the invasion of the Normans who immediately formed the ruling class. The history that was taught (until the last thirty years when German and French curricula were shifted substantially to include more critical viewpoints) was the history of victory. How many of us, I wonder, taught before the 1970s were told about the battles our nation lost through incompetence or weakness, the harm we inflicted on other people as we subjugated them – not in other continents (that is well covered in the guilt-ridden classes of the post-imperial period) but near home, the skirmishes and local slaughters that marked out the petty boundaries of our lands and culture, and how many fewer are taught about other peoples' battles, origins and development which did not impinge on us at all? It did, of course, but the links were too subtle for the direct relation of history as seen through the linear historian's mind. The causes and effects that really guided events were often very different from those handed down as official history.

We need a new version of history as our standard, one that is more complex and therefore more accurate. UNESCO has realized this, commissioning many volumes to present the world from a viewpoint that does not take sides. So has the Council of Europe which has tried over many years too. That, though, has proved to be a worthy but as yet unrewarding effort with results which are at best patchy and confined to those countries which have for the most part stood aside from the colonialist era or which have been caught in the middle of the bigger competing powers. Instead the demands of insecure local nationalism are urging that history be returned to the comforting picture of winners and losers as portrayed to previous generations. In part they have a point. The social movement, lifestyle before events, approach that has shaped history teaching since the 1960s was more a response to Marxism and the increasing dominance of economics. It was also a way of dealing with the collapse of empire. It was not possible to pretend that our history was not a messy succession of inexcusable events so the events themselves were downgraded into minor occurrences, inevitable in the sociological record.

To that extent the nationalists are right. We do need to grasp the chronology that has shaped Europe. Where they are wrong is in believing that by isolating history to fit the aspirations of an individual nation its long-term future is well served. History, whether it be about events or the forces that made them occur, needs to be communicated so that it provides a European consciousness, an understanding of the similarities and discrepancies that led people to behave as they did. Only then will the basic foundations have been laid for generations to grow up thinking as Europeans in spirit as well as according to their official documents.

Literature too must be made available in a more open-handed way. It is still remarkably difficult, indeed almost commercially impossible, to publish a book simultaneously across Europe. Absurdly in the age of the Internet there is no pan-European publishing house, even for major works in the main languages. It is hardly surprising, therefore, that the teachers of literature should concentrate so much on national literature or on that of the main cultural groups. The European Union has recognized the principle of helping the translation of works written in languages spoken by comparatively few people. Mostly, however, this involves translating them into one of the major languages:

Dutch to Spanish or Gaelic to German, for example. This is a start, but it would be perhaps even more rewarding to translate the works into languages representing cultures sharing a similar sense of being undervalued; Slovene to Welsh, for example or Finnish to Basque. Then it would only be right to banish the assumption that it was necessary to learn a major language in order to have access to its literature. Italian works need to appear as much in Norwegian or Slovakian as the other way round. Ideally, of course, we would all have the linguistic skills to read and enjoy the literature in its original tongue and, travelling among those who one could describe as professional Europeans, one will meet the occasional astonishing linguist happy to traverse eight or nine languages instead of the more usual two or three in comfort. However children who are not travelling constantly cannot be expected to do so. Education must play its part, therefore, and the breadth of European writing must be the basis of teaching. Now, instead of classes calling themselves Literature lessons, they are English or French or Welsh or Portuguese, depending on the home country. The result is that by the age of eighteen children in England have read Jane Austen but not Cervantes, in France Rimbaud but not Blake, in Italy Boito but not Dinesen. The teaching of literature and history must be made to take the same universal approach as is taken in physics, music or environmental studies.

The problem with education is that once people have passed through its formal stages its influence, as with all other experiences, can and will wane. The process of maturity is, thank goodness, only just beginning when most people leave education. While many continue to study later in life or retrain, learning new skills to augment their professional abilities, there is a point at which the lessons imbued at school and university become no more than a background. The influence is deep, though, and it can provide a guide to the character and approach that inform later decisions. That is why it is so important to instil the spirit of generosity towards Europe. However, by the time adults are in a position to have a significant influence on political, academic and social thought, there will be many other factors coming into play.

Daily education in adulthood (in the broad sense that I have used it, deriving from its Latin root meaning a 'leading out') is largely conducted by the press. Although television is a good medium for the delivery of news (and occasionally for head-to-head debate) newspapers, the radio and magazines remain the real agents for forming and sometimes fermenting opinions. Such continent-wide newspapers as do exist have so far had only partial success. The Americans, paradoxically often the first to see Europe as a single entity – a mirror image of their own country, perhaps but a distorted one – have had the Herald Tribune, edited in Paris, as a European paper for several decades. The newer, weekly, European, started by that peculiar combination of visionary and fraudster, Robert Maxwell, and now owned by the Barclay brothers (who live on one of the Channel Islands outside the framework of the Union, again a neat paradox) has yet to establish a secure place in the market. Otherwise the distribution of the main national papers to most parts of the continent has created a greater sense of belonging to the daily reality of Europe than any single piece of legislation. Corriere della Serra, Le Monde, El Pais, Frankfurter Algemeine Zeitung, Volkskrant and The Guardian are now visible on most high streets every morning – and increasingly on the same day, removing the old feeling of 'being abroad' created by glimpsing the news from home a day late.

This wider distribution is only a matter of the exporting of national views, however, and for a real sense of integration there needs to be a different approach. A true European newspaper, daily and in at least three languages, would be a emblematic gesture but would have a doubtful circulation base except among the most die-hard enthusiasts of integration. There is also a sense that in downgrading the influence and respect of the principal national journals a measure of cultural pride would be lost and resentment cultivated. A more promising initiative would be a more comprehensive version of that attempted by six newspapers in the late 1980s, among them El Pais, The Independent (London) and La Republica. This allowed important articles originating in one paper to be translated and included in all the others, creating a series of perspectives different from those usually associated with each paper. This had the advantage of showing how individuals (and publishers) which had roughly similar political standpoints could nonetheless approach items of news with markedly different national attitudes. A community spirit, entering debate without antagonism, was the illuminating result.

There is room for the project to be revived and extended. Indeed there would be room for the newspaper publishers, the European Broadcasting Union, the Council of Europe's Cultural Division and the European Union's DGX to join forces to promote the idea for journals and radio stations, covering the political spectrum as well as geographical states. The town-twinning programmes similarly could be used to create links between local papers and the regional ones: The Scotsman (Edinburgh) and La Nazione (Firenze), for example. As well as giving citizens a useful view of Europe with connections to their own but with a wider sense of reference, it would allow alliances to grow up within the media at the programming and editorial level without risking a concentration of ownership. So far it is to the benefit of European diversity and cultural pluralism that the big conglomerates that threaten to undermine democratic control in television, and the news media of individual nations, have not moved onto the European stage.

While European consciousness is to be encouraged and applauded it must not be at the cost of letting tycoons like Silvio Berlusconi and Rupert Murdoch, who so dominate the media in Italy and the UK, extend their empires beyond a certain limit. That limit is the line between allowing freedom of commercial growth (and the right to propagate one's opinions wherever and howsoever one wishes) and the right of societies to protect themselves against a dangerous shrinkage in the breadth of intellectual and political opinion on offer to the citizen. It will be necessary to legislate on a European basis if any of the press barons show a taste for concentrating their power by acquiring a significant proportion of the newspaper titles. Enforcing strict anti-monopolist rules across the media will be the only way of safeguarding cultural and political pluralism. Ownership is not the same as shared interest, however, and the wider circulation of ideas around the continent is an important element in building the layers of a shared cultural consciousness. Musicians, scientists and painters have always operated on this assumption, after all.

The arts have a vital role to play in the building process but it is not the affirmation role that politicians – and indeed many who are their followers – often assume it to be. Most of the arts are bad at answering questions. Solutions are sometimes inspired but, unlike science, rarely have a bedrock of proof. In the main the arts are there to question, sometimes gently, sometimes sharply. Their validity comes through their ability to use forms of entertainment to help people think about themselves and the world they live in. When the arts preach they are usually no more interesting than the dogmatists of religion and politics. When they reflect in a quizzical way or move so that the usual imperatives of life are suspended for a moment, then they are able to change society. It is important to realize, though, that the artists do not make the change. They are the agents of change. They stir the resolve of people to make changes themselves. For the most part even the most revolutionary of artistic endeavours will have only a mild effect. A person may experience a cathartic moment of release when hearing a magnificent performance of a Mahler symphony or be inspired to find reconciliation by the final moments of *The Winter's Tale* but the moment will be short-lived unless the resolution was there in embryo form already. The arts can fertilize the embryo of change, they cannot be change itself. However, if no change is envisaged by the artists then art is not involved either. The process is then one of artifice only, of decoration. The entertainer works to confirm assumptions, to make people feel comfortable with the passage of their lives, to enhance their enjoyment. There is nothing wrong with this, and life would be a miserable experience without it, but it should not be confused with the more purposeful nature of art.

Politics is firmly on the side of entertainment. Like entertainers politicians see their role as deliverers of contentment. They like to believe that they have at least some of the answers to existing in a state of placid prosperity, if not always of active happiness. The arts at their best are therefore always going to be uncomfortable, subversive of the serenity which politicians like to see. For this reason it can be said that comedians and some rock musicians are often more truly artists than many painters and sculptors. To be in the service of the state or of a group of citizens, the establishment, is something that artists should accept only on the understanding that their subversive questioning is the function required. The glorification of a civic project, the praise of authority, the ratification of official policy is the job of the courtier and the artisan. The subject may be worthy of the praise and delivering it may be an honourable task but it is not something the artist should be on the payroll to do.

Without intensive questioning and continuous subversion, however, society cannot move forward. The arts and opposition politicians are in the same business, therefore, and a democratic society which believes in its own intent to progress, cannot do without either of them. A society that did would soon stagnate and its citizens would not tolerate its institutions except as a result of fear (or massive bribery). In a sense it is a misnomer to equate the arts and culture. The arts, like politics, are the means by which a culture develops and expresses its fears and desires. They have much in common but they are not culture itself. It is for this reason that I have left discussion of their role to such a late stage of this book. However, for a culture to be said to exist, let alone thrive, the arts must be an essential part of its make-up. A culture bereft of its arts is little more than a scrap yard for human machinery.

They are certainly an indispensable element in any programme to build a European consciousness. Apart from their obvious suitability for the task in terms of natural mobility, general acceptance and unthreatening nature, the arts have one strong claim on the purse of European governments. Alone of all the spheres of activity on offer they deliver benefits across all the categories desired by society; they enable citizens to articulate their perceptions; they encourage visions of culture that can be transplanted across boundaries and they are instruments for education, employment, tourism, the banishment of alienation, economic success in technologically advanced industries and the environmentally acceptable rejuvenation of rural and urban communities. For all these reasons the arts deserve a far more exalted place in the budgetary decisions of states and European institutions alike.

Any European body which invests generously in the arts will find the return remarkable compared to its other programmes. Only, however, if the investment is principally in people rather than buildings. Traditionally all official entities find building investment easier to fit into the models of their professional world than artistic activity. Buildings have a limited cost which is relatively predictable and finite. They are left behind as durable demonstrations of the far-sightedness of the investing authority. They do not ask difficult questions or bite back. They do not travel either, however, so for European institutions the benefit they can deliver to the aim of developing a cultural consciousness that is friendly to the ideal of Europe is strictly limited. Instead of spending huge amounts of common finance on new buildings, except as an integral part of infrastructure development and the preservation of the heritage, the European institutions should leave buildings to the discretion of the states and invest in activity instead.

There are many ways of helping the arts to bind Europe. For the performing arts and exhibitions a large budget needs to be available to cope with the costs of partnership between cultural regions (even within the same nation state: Brittany and Provence are culturally far enough apart to be foreigners to each other). Trans-national projects in publishing and radio need the same degree of help for creative development that takes them outside their rigid language groups. Co-production in all areas would be helped enormously if the invested funds from continental, national and local authorities could be swapped between partners in projects. The most pressing problem for artists and their organizations – the cost of travel and accommodation in Europe – could be addressed with a voucher scheme redeemable with airlines and hotel chains which, almost alone in industry, work, like artists, in many countries. The mobility of audiences and visitors is important too and so much more could be made of the links between cultures if those links were extensively built into travel packages. The Council of Europe made a start with its cultural routes programme but, although imaginative, it was never marketed and promoted with the vigour and professional-ism needed to make a mark in the travel industry.

Such ideas are obvious ways in which the tentative efforts of Europe's supranational institutions can be extended and deepened into a policy which matches the aspirations of the cultural clause of the Maastricht Treaty and the old, and largely disregarded, cultural convention of the Council of Europe. They all depend, however, on the basic notion that it is worthwhile, indeed imperative, to allocate an adequate level of funds to make sense of the assertion that culture is central to European development.

It is not enough, however, to give money to the manifestations of culture as they have been understood since the romantic period. In any case it is increasingly plain that the boundary between arts and science, so rigorously enforced in the nineteenth and twentieth centuries, is a false one. Far more useful is the sixteenth-and seventeenth-century confusion between the two, when one could talk quite comfortably about the art of astronomy and the science of music. The boundaries between the academic disciplines of philosophy, history, archaeology, anthropology and the performing and visual arts are equally unhelpful, of use only to those seeking to define themselves restrictively. And if these limits on the contemplative side of human life are to be blurred and breached, then it is necessary too to recognize the points of stress in the cultural landscape which release energy but which also cause Europe to buckle and erupt so often. These have little to do with art or science – though they can be relieved by them.

The politicians and officials who crave for a continent they can control will never wholly succeed, thank heavens. The spirit of the people of Europe will not submit for long to the rules and regulations that colourless leaders impose ever more frantically as they strive to retain their balance. Merging the money, harmonising the shape of cucumbers or the gauge of rails or the design of tax forms will throw up as many problems as it solves. Each attempt to bind Europe with economic theory has always led to war and catastrophe in the past because the theory was always thought to be all-embracing; more cogent that the combined interests of the nations on which it was foisted. The forced merger of Europe through a central alliance that carries, at best, only the grudging support of its people, anxious to at least try believing what their bullying Chancellors and Presidents say, will soon prove as unhappy as all the rest unless the time and trouble is taken to put cultural security as high as physical and financial security on the list of objectives.

Culture is the bedrock of Europe. It is its source of strength, passion, variety and excitement. From its wine to its symphony orchestras Europe has inspired the world even as it conquered and exploited. Where the empires of Europe have left anything positive behind it has been the legacy of ancient Greece, in its architecture and the echoes of its political experiments with democracy, and the remnants of culture; the forms of European dress, music, theatre and poetry.

Europe, though, has too often paid lip service to its culture without understanding it. The web of allegiances that entangles each individual; the network of loyalties, fears, grievances and myths by which nation and sub-nation defines itself; the potential for expression in the citizen as an essential part of a satisfactory human life; the boundless goodwill and rich enlightenment which exists alongside and interwoven with fear, prejudice and mistrust: all are the fissured sediments and compacted minerals which have made Europe such an exasperating but astonishing place to live for the last three thousand years.

The people of Europe have had more impact, for bad and good, on the world than those of any other continent. People from every other continent now live in Europe, call it home and think of themselves as European. Trying to pretend that we can fit into a neat and bland design will only exacerbate the divisions. We will perpetually feel compelled to compete with as much aggression as we feel is necessary to exert our individuality, whether as men and women, ethnic groups, social classes, professionals or nationalities. If we are to form a benevolent concept of Europe that will last, one which can stand the strains of the bad economic cycle as well as the good, one capable of including all its inhabitants without fear or disadvantage, then we must learn to agree about how those who administer our lives are organized.

Europe's troubles begin and end with disputes about who has the right to take decisions that affect our lives. Often we are willing to cede control but only if we feel confident that those to whom we cede it understand and appreciate the forces that shape us.

This is our cultural landscape. The success or failure of politics is in its gift. We have the resources and the cleverness to preserve and nurture it. Our cultural security holds the promise of a century free of the brutality and megalomania which has ruined so many. We owe it to ourselves.

Coda

'If, thanks to Peter the Great, we have been fatally caught on the tail of Europe, then so we shall remain forever ... for, born Russians, we are at the same time even far more Europeans and we have so resolutely and deeply fostered and assimilated their forms that to tear ourselves from them we would have to strain and do violence to ourselves, and from such straining and violence nothing artistic could come. Where there is violence there is no inspiration, and where there is no inspiration there is no art.'

Pyotr Ilyich Tchaikovsky
Letter to Sergei Taneyev,
13 August 1880